ObamaCare *Simplified*

ObamaCare
SIMPLIFIED

A Clear Guide to Making ObamaCare Work for You

Zephyros Press

ISBN: Print 978-1-62315-252-9 | eBook 978-1-62315-275-8

Do you have health insurance?

Employer Insurance

> If you are satisfied, you may continue your present insurance. If you are unsatisfied, you may modify it during any offered open enrollment period. You may also be able to buy Marketplace insurance, or you can wait for likely ACA-driven changes to your employer's offerings by 2017. **SEE CHAPTERS 15, 16, AND 17.**

Private Insurance

> Typically you may keep your present coverage. If you are unsatisfied, you may be able to switch to Marketplace insurance or modify your insurance during an open enrollment period. **SEE CHAPTERS 8, 9, AND 14.**

Medicare, Medicaid, CHIP, or TRICARE*

> Enrollees in these programs keep their current coverage; they are exempt from any requirement to buy insurance for themselves. Benefits provided by these programs make them ACA-compliant.

Check to see if your program covers dependent members of your household. If it does not, the ACA requires that the uninsured household members get coverage or insurance.

SEE CHAPTERS 7, 12, 13, AND 21.

Veterans benefits other than TRICARE

> Your program may or may not satisfy the requirement; check at www.healthcare.gov or with the Department of Veterans Affairs. **SEE CHAPTER 7.**

You MUST get insurance unless you qualify for an <u>exemption</u> because:

> You have religious reasons not to comply. **SEE CHAPTERS 7, 14, AND 22.**

> You are eligible for care through the Indian Health Service. **SEE CHAPTER 14.**

> You are unemployed. *You are exempt for up to three months.* **SEE CHAPTER 18.**

> You are an unauthorized immigrant. *You are barred from all Marketplace subsidies and nearly all expanded Medicaid benefits, as well as the insurance purchase mandate.* **SEE CHAPTER 24.**

> You cannot afford it. *If you earn less than the lower limit for filing income taxes, or if your out-of-pocket premium costs are more than 8 percent of your income, you are exempt.* **SEE CHAPTERS 5, 10, 17, 21, AND 22.**

Do you qualify for expanded Medicaid? If your income is at or below 133 percent of the federal poverty level, you qualify for Medicaid. If your state is participating in expanded Medicaid, you may apply for Medicaid. **SEE CHAPTERS 1, 2, 3, 4, 21, AND 23.**

Are you eligible for Marketplace subsidies? If your income is between 133 percent and 400 percent of the federal poverty level, you qualify for a Marketplace premium subsidy. If your income is up to 250 percent of federal poverty level, you may also qualify for "cost sharing" subsidies for out-of-pocket charges. **SEE CHAPTERS 7, 10, AND 21.**

Contents

Introduction

After a bloody legislative fight in Congress, the Patient Protection and Affordable Care Act (PPACA) or Affordable Care Act (ACA), for short, was passed in the spring of 2010. Health care reform had been a major issue in the 2008 election, and the act finally squeaked through a strongly divided Congress. For at least a year, partisans on both sides of the aisle had fed the media with hyperbolic pronouncements that the bill would destroy America or save it, depending on which cable channel you watched. President Obama signed it into law on March 23, 2010.

Almost immediately, it became clear that the law needed tweaking, and a series of amendments were signed by the president a week later as the Health Care and Education Reconciliation Act of 2010. These two laws were designed to remake how health care was paid for in the United States. The combination is what we now refer to as Obamacare. (*Note: The nickname* Obamacare *started as a pejorative term. However, President Obama has adopted it himself, so we use it throughout this book.*)

OVER TWENTY-FOUR HUNDRED PAGES

For the man on the street, one fact about Obamacare stands out: it's complex. The oft-quoted statistic is that the 2,400 pages are impossible to decipher, much less understand. The situation is even worse if we add the rules needed to apply the law. Estimates run from a conservative 9,000 or so pages (*The Washington Post*) to a whopping 33,000 (Senator Mitch McConnell). Is it even possible to come to grips with all this?

The reason the act is so huge, dense and indecipherable, springs from the current intricacies of government-funded health care. If you read the actual Affordable Care Act, you'll run immediately into things like this (from page 117):

(2) INDIVIDUALS ELIGIBLE FOR ENROLLMENT—An individual is described in this paragraph for any plan year if the individual (A) has not attained the age of 30 before the beginning of the plan year; or (B) has a certification in effect for any plan year under this title that the individual is exempt from the requirement under section 5000A of the Internal Revenue Code of 1986 by reason of (i) section 5000A(e)(1) of such Code (relating to individuals without affordable coverage); or (ii) section 5000A(e)(5) of such Code (relating to individuals with hardships).

The confusion comes because most of the act references other sections of law to make changes needed and to avoid conflicts. It is largely regulations about regulations.

We'll resolve this difficulty in two ways. The first is to pull back and get a broad overview of what the legislation is supposed to accomplish, how it changes the current health care system, and how Obamacare is structured. The second way we'll make it understandable is to focus directly on specific situations—you don't need to be an expert on the whole system to figure out how you and your loved ones will be affected.

HOW THIS BOOK IS ORGANIZED

Part I describes the existing health care system and gives the context for the changes that come with Obamacare. With this background on how health care is structured in America, it's much easier to see what Obamacare is meant to accomplish and how it goes about it. Plus, it's an interesting story.

Part II looks at Obamacare in a general way—the structure and high-lights. This is the "how it works" section, where we explain the individual mandate, insurance exchanges, and how things are supposed to be funded. Here you will also find a timeline that shows when each of the major provisions kicks in, and the best information available at the time of publication on getting ready to comply with the individual mandate in the new insurance marketplace.

Part III covers specifics that will put the spotlight on different categories. There are key differences in how Obamacare affects citizens, depending on age, income, and employment status. Also included is a glossary of terms and a guide to help you with frequently asked questions.

ABOUT THE TONE OF THE BOOK

This book isn't meant to be a political screed. We've tried very hard to remain neutral—for good reason. Obamacare is a fact. Like it or not, it's the current law of the land. Navigating the new terrain is hard enough without getting bogged down in opinion and controversy, and this book draws a detailed map to follow, leaving politics out of the mix.

Where there is strong disagreement, we've provided both sides of the issue, and we leave it to readers to form their own conclusions.

Make no mistake, though; there are winners and losers under Obamacare. These include not just individual citizens but businesses and health care providers as well. It is also open to modification, and as of September 2013, there have been forty-one attempts in the House to repeal the law. So far, Obamacare has survived not only these but a Supreme Court challenge as well.

Will it be modified? Almost certainly. As the provisions come online, citizens will feel a real impact, both in their wallets and in the experiences they have with their caregivers. We are a vocal bunch in the United States, and when we get our backs up, we vote for change. Just what those changes will be, no one can say right now. But being well informed on Obamacare will empower you to make clear decisions that consider the purposes, funding issues, and outcomes of the law. An educated voter is a wise voter.

Beyond this, we believe that becoming an informed health care consumer leads to better overall outcomes. Even those who avoid medical care as a rule will eventually need treatment. No one stays healthy forever. By learning what is and isn't covered (or how to find out in your circumstances), you will be able to access the system for your own benefit at the lowest cost and with the least amount of trouble.

Those who are currently receiving medical care will also benefit from understanding how Obamacare will affect them. Adapting to the new conditions comes with a certain amount of anxiety, but this can be minimized. You don't have to feel as if it's too complex and that you are without options. Knowledge really is a powerful thing. So let's get started.

PART I

Getting Started with Health Care

CHAPTER 1

Health Care in the United States

Understanding the changes coming under the Affordable Care Act (ACA) means coming to grips with how health care services are currently delivered in the United States, including health insurance and who pays for it. Whether you agree or disagree with the politics behind Obamacare, the legislation doesn't create a completely new way of doing business. Rather, it modifies the current system in some key ways.

HOW DID WE GET HERE?

Seeing the big picture of health care in the United States today will help you understand what Obamacare attempts to accomplish and why.

Fee-for-Service

The idea of health insurance didn't catch on in the United States until more than a hundred years after the country was founded. Before the early 1900s, almost everyone in the country paid for the health services they received just as we now pay for any other professional service: you paid for what you got.

This so-called *fee-for-service* model is still around in health care, but it finds fewer and fewer applications, primarily because medical care costs so much. Also called *pay-as-you-go*, we commonly run into fee-for-service when treatment is rendered outside the scope of our health insurance. Simply put, a fee-for-service relationship occurs when the patient pays all the costs for an appointment or treatment. It's the easiest model to understand: you get X services and pay Y dollars, with no insurance involved at all.

The Rise of Prepaid Services

What we now call health insurance started out as prepayment for services and was tied to specific hospitals. As early as 1911, hospitals were large enough that they worried about keeping their beds occupied. One way to do this was to accept payment for services to be delivered later, in effect, using the same "pay first, get benefits later" idea that you find at the root of all insurance policies.

There were several advantages for the hospital that offered prepayments: They could better moderate their cash flow with ongoing, smaller payments. They were able to reduce collections, since patients would already have some money paid in. They could keep patients from shopping around because subscribers had to use their facility to use the insurance.

Blue Cross started this way in 1929, in Dallas, Texas. By paying six dollars a year, Baylor University teachers could receive twenty-one days of health care. The idea caught on and hospitals across the United States started using it. Another version, Blue Shield, arose a decade later with employee groups contracting with physicians directly instead of being hospital based. The two weren't merged until 1982.

These primitive forms of health care coverage demonstrate some themes we still deal with today. Some key differences between fee-for-service and insurance are outlined in the table on the following page.

FEE-FOR-SERVICE VERSUS INSURANCE

Fee-for-Service	Early Insurance
Patients pay everything, but only when they need care	Patients still pay, but in smaller amounts and before services are rendered
Money moves in lumps, depending on need	Money moves all the time, irrespective of need
Patients shop for services	Patients are bound to a provider
Money is directly tied to need	Money is disconnected from need, yielding winners and losers
No payment or profit without using services	Payments and profits stem from signing up more subscribers

Two important features emerge here. The first is that with insurance, subscribers are "captured." They will use the services of whoever honors their policy. This reduces competition between providers of health care and places free market forces one step removed from the transaction. The second feature is that insurance generates its own profit.

For-Profit Insurance

Insurance is sold based on a prediction of future need. This is an inexact science, and to make sure less is paid out (to the pool of insured) than is taken in (from premiums), an *overage* is added. If they estimate that a hospital will have to deliver one thousand babies next year, they want to make sure they take in enough premiums to cover at least that much. Otherwise they will lose money. The easiest way to do this is to charge a bit more than they think will cover the costs. If this overage isn't used up, they get to keep it, along with any profit margin already built into policies.

In our economic system, money flow determines what emerges and what is tossed aside. And by the 1930s, insurance for health care was here to stay, offering patients a way to avoid crippling financial damage, and offering hospitals or doctor groups a way to not just manage cash flow but also to generate profits independent of services rendered.

Nonprofit Insurance

The main difference between for-profit and nonprofit health insurance is who gets the money. A nonprofit enterprise is restricted in how it is able to spend money that accrues, being generally limited to infrastructure and salaries, although many nonprofits also spend on charitable works.

There are no shareholders in nonprofit enterprises, and no dividends are paid. They also have a preferred tax status and can avoid the taxes a for-profit enterprise must pay. However, it is a mistake to think nonprofits aren't generating money or that they will necessarily offer better deals to policyholders. Nonprofits face the same challenges that for-profit insurers do, in addition to often adopting the role as insurer for less profitable sectors of the economy. Still, a 2012 *Consumer Reports* survey ranked nonprofits ahead of others in the health care insurance market, with top marks going to Kaiser Permanente.

Third-Party Payers

In its earliest version, prepayment for services had only two parties in the transaction: the hospital and the public. Very quickly, experts in the insurance field stepped in as intermediaries. They brought financial expertise and knowledge of the industry. They also brought in marketing skills, enabling a broadening of subscribers and the advantages of economies of scale.

The new relationship added insurance companies as third parties who stood between the public and the medical community, at least as far as payment was concerned. They negotiated with policyholders and competed with each other to offer acceptable rates and coverage. They also negotiated for the lowest prices they could get from health care providers. The difference between the price they purchased health care for and what they sold it for became their profit margins.

Again, money is important here. Insurance companies succeed or fail based on the simple difference between money collected from policyholders and money paid out to hospitals and doctors and for other covered services. But there's an added element.

When an insurer has a large client base, it has economic power. This can be used to negotiate for lower prices from health care providers. If an insurer can guarantee a certain level of "business" to a hospital, it can then ask for (and get) a discount based on this volume. However, by inserting themselves between the patients and their treatment, insurers can also influence not only what care is paid for but the circumstances under which payments are made. Patients are no longer free to get whatever they want, whenever they want it, since the patient no longer pays the bills directly. This is an important principle we will return to again and again: the concept of limits and scarcity. For now, it's enough to see that there are limits built into the system.

Government Rulings and Employer-Sponsored Insurance

In one sense, government regulation has always been a part of health care delivery. From licensing doctors to accrediting hospitals, and everything U.S. health care has, we've always had some oversight from government. The roots of the Food and Drug Administration (FDA) go back to the late nineteenth century, and while there still wasn't much federal regulation on health care in the 1930s, state-level regulations existed.

A key development in health insurance sprang from a minor ruling during Franklin D. Roosevelt's administration. In the late 1930s and into the

1940s, the United States was moving out of the Great Depression and into World War II. One of the consequences of the war was a labor shortage. The war was draining so much labor that wages were at risk of skyrocketing beyond the economy's ability to control. Fearing wage inflation, President Roosevelt and a willing Congress put in place wage freezes to head off a round of spiraling competition between employers hiring from a smaller and smaller labor pool. This was also when women were first broadly tapped as a resource in the labor market, for the same reason.

The minor ruling that would kick-start health care insurance as we know it today came from the War Labor Board, the institution that oversaw and regulated wages. They decided that fringe benefits (like health insurance) didn't count as wages when calculating compensation. This meant an employer could attract needed workers not by raising wages (which was regulated), but by offering heath insurance as part of the compensation package.

Suddenly, third-party insurance was a hot commodity. The new customer was now the employer who wanted to offer benefit packages. Adding this fourth party to the mix of hospitals, the public, and insurance companies complicated the landscape a bit more.

A second ruling made after the war, this time by the National Labor Relations Board (the body governing workers' rights and unions) boosted employer-sponsored health insurance. The board decided that benefit packages, including insurance, could be part of the collective bargaining process. Unions would thereafter press for better coverage when negotiating contracts. And finally in 1954, the IRS stepped in and ruled that health insurance premiums were not taxable.

These three developments, over less than two decades, shaped a huge swath of the private insurance landscape, creating much of what we see today. While not directly regulating health care, the effect of the regulations was a proliferation of privately funded, employer-linked health plans. This is why insurance and employment are bound together so tightly today. Employers saved money and paid less in taxes while being able to offer more to attract workers. Employees could negotiate for better coverage and not have to pay the premiums themselves.

It all worked well, as long as employment was high. There were still holes in the system, and in the 1960s, these would be addressed by Medicare and Medicaid.

GOVERNMENT-SPONSORED HEALTH CARE

Government-sponsored health care plans are those that are sponsored by either the state or the federal government.

Social Security

Social Security was enacted during FDR's administration as part of the New Deal legislation designed to provide a "safety net" for aged Americans. Although health care provisions were planned for the legislation, the version that passed did not include health insurance. It wouldn't be until 1965 that amendments to the Social Security Act added Medicare and Medicaid.

Medicare and Medicaid

These two programs were enacted under President Lyndon Johnson's administration as additions to the Social Security Act. Both are meant to provide health care to underserved populations: Medicare for retirees (seniors over sixty-five) and Medicaid for the impoverished. (A way to remember the difference: MedicaRE = REtired; MedicaID = Income Dependent.)

Medicare is a benefit all seniors are eligible for, regardless of their income, so long as they meet a few key conditions:

- They are or have been U.S. citizens or permanent legal residents for at least five continuous years.
- They are sixty-five years old or older.
- They or their spouse has met employment/payroll requirements (ten years of contributions). Those who do not have enough work history to qualify are still eligible for Medicare, but they have to pay premiums based on their contributions while employed.

As part of Social Security, a portion of wages are collected (and matched by employers) to fund the program. A total contribution of 2.9 percent of income is taken (1.45 percent each from employees and employers). This amount is then used to fund Medicare Part A, which is called the *hospital insurance* portion. In 2013, the percentage collected will rise on income over $200,000 for an individual ($250,000 for couples) to 3.8 percent.

Medicare Part A covers hospitalization, with the first sixty days covered fully and an additional month covered with a co-pay (currently $289 per day). The other "parts" of Medicare include the following:

- **Part B**, which covers outpatient medical care and some testing. After meeting a deductible of $140 a year, enrollees are then eligible for an 80–20 split of costs, with the government picking up the larger portion.
- **Part C**, which is a blend of publicly and privately funded insurance. While complex, the basic idea is to use the money that would otherwise come from Part A and Part B to fund a private health insurance plan. Any plan offered must at least meet the benefits under "regular" Medicare but can increase premiums for additional benefits, such as prescription drugs, vision, or dental care.
- **Part D**, which is the most recent change, offers a prescription drug benefit to anyone enrolled in Parts A and B. The program is not standardized. The costs and benefits vary, depending on the choices patients wish to make.

Medicaid, the second major government-administered health insurance attached to the Social Security Act in 1965, is designed to meet the needs of the poor. It is an entitlement program that attempts to support state efforts to pay the medical expenses of low-income citizens.

As a blend of federal and state programs, Medicaid can vary in benefits and administration, and criteria for eligibility. It works by providing matching funds to states that participate and meet minimum federal guidelines. Obamacare originally required that income eligibility would extend to those making 133 percent of the federal poverty level (FPL). (The actual dollar amount varies by the number of children and local cost of living.)

This expansion of services as a federal requirement imposed on states was the subject of a Supreme Court case, as some states didn't want to be forced to comply. By increasing the number of eligible Medicaid recipients, states would have to match federal funds for considerably more people—something many states objected to in times of tight budgets. The states won the court challenge, and they are not required to match funds to meet the new standards if they choose not to. To keep things on track, the federal government responded by offering to pay whatever the difference was to cover this new demographic, instead of requiring states to pay half.

The current plan is for the federal government to pay for eligibility expansion on a descending scale, with percentages decreasing from 100 percent for the first three years, down to 90 percent by 2020, where it will stay from then on. This amount is just for those who become eligible under Obamacare, not for those who would already be eligible based on income or infirmity in their state. Twenty-four states and the District of Columbia have accepted either the original federal mandate or the post-court-decision sweetened deal. Observers typically cite twenty-one states as having rejected the expansion of Medicaid, whether by legislative prohibition, governor's veto, or other means. The remaining states are in some form of debate or consideration of expansion. It is worth noting that these last two categories are both subject to change in response to shifting political winds within each state.

As will be discussed further, low-income residents of states without expanded Medicare coverage will not gain any new opportunities to insure themselves from Obamacare. Their access to health care will be much the same as it is today.

Other Programs of Note

While Medicare and Medicaid provide government-paid insurance directly, other acts have modified how health insurance plans are administered and taxed. These do not shoulder the burden of funding directly, but do shape the marketplace by regulating what can and cannot be offered.

For example, the Employment Retirement and Security Act included provisions on what constituted minimum standards on what employers could offer as a qualified pension plan. Enacted in 1974 under President Nixon, this act was modified during the Reagan administration by the Consolidated Omnibus Budget Reconciliation Act (COBRA) and further modified under the Obama presidency.

COBRA allows employees who become unemployed under certain circumstances to maintain the health insurance they had while working. It is administered as a tax imposed on employers if they do not maintain a qualifying insurance plan or if the employer offers health care and has at least twenty employees.

Using a penalty is another way to modify employer behavior without directly mandating it. This same mechanism is in play under Obamacare, where employers who do not offer qualifying plans will be penalized by paying additional taxes.

COBRA allowed employees to keep their health insurance current by paying the premiums themselves, but after a job loss, most didn't take the option. Estimates were that less than 10 percent of those eligible for COBRA took advantage of it, and in 2009, legislation was passed that would pay up to 65 percent of the premiums for those recently unemployed. In any case, COBRA provisions were never meant to be long-term, extending the ability to keep insurance for only eighteen months.

The underutilization of COBRA illustrates another key theme in U.S. health care. When patients have to pay, they use less health care and will sometimes forego coverage. Taking on the premiums themselves, rather than having an employer pay, led to most unemployed workers simply dropping coverage altogether.

One other provision included in COBRA is worth noting. The Emergency Medical Treatment and Active Labor Act was included as part of the overall legislation. This mandates that hospitals provide emergency care to anyone who shows up at the emergency room (ER). ERs cannot discriminate based on a patient's legal status—for instance, they cannot deny health care to people residing in the United States without legal authorization—nor can ERs deny care based on a patient's ability to pay. This has made the emergency room a kind of last resort for those without insurance or a primary-care physician. This mandate is often cited as a burden on hospitals, since they have to provide services for which they may never collect any fees. Some hospitals have dropped their emergency rooms because of it.

HMOs

Health Maintenance Organizations (HMOs) differ from other types of plans because they focus on preventive care and keeping all services in a cost-controlled network of providers. There have been a few legislative attempts to bring this model to prominence, but in the case of HMOs, government has been less successful in changing the behavior of the health insurance marketplace.

A classic HMO harks back to the first type of health insurance covered in this chapter: the prepaid model used by hospitals in the early 1900s. The HMO collects money on a set per patient basis, and then has to provide services when the patient gets ill, without regard to the cost of treatment.

These organizations are called are call "health maintenance" because it pays to keep patients well. By focusing on preventive care, an HMO could reduce long-term costs—disease could be caught early and managed more efficiently.

Under Nixon, a program was started to offer subsidies to qualified HMO-style insurance and change state-level regulations that limited HMOs. The Health Maintenance Organization Act of 1973 had one key provision—employers that offered health insurance also had to offer at least one qualifying HMO employees could choose. Unfortunately, this didn't have the expected results, since HMOs were not available everywhere and patients were often dissatisfied with the plans. Some balked at having to stay "in network" for all services, and others complained about HMOs' cost-cutting practices when they didn't get the attention or services they were used to. The mandated "dual choice" provision has expired and employers are no longer required to offer HMO coverage beside other plans.

The HMO model also formed the basis for another failed attempt to modify how health care is financed in the United States. In 1993, the Clinton administration promoted the Health Security Act, a type of mandated, universal coverage based on HMOs. The act failed to gain enough support and didn't pass Congress. Called "Hillarycare," the act would have required all employers to offer HMO-style insurance policies to their workers. Some elements of this have returned in Obamacare.

While HMO coverage is not mandated in Obamacare, some of the ideas are—ideas that hark back to Nixon. The primary reason is that preventive care, including screening, has been shown to reduce overall health care costs. The easiest place to see this is with vaccinations. At a couple of dollars per person, diseases like polio or measles can be prevented. However, holding off until treatment is needed often entails expensive and sometimes lifelong treatment.

Studies show that screening for disease conditions can yield the same benefits—not only do patients have better outcomes overall, but early detection and treatment costs less. Money is a huge consideration in health care. Efficiencies pay off, not just in overall expenditures but by allowing the same funds to cover more of those who cannot afford to pay.

Current estimates of health care costs in the United States vary by calculation method, with elements like lost work days counted or not, depending on who is adding up the numbers. But a conservative estimate of expenditures easily surpasses 15 percent of the gross domestic product (GDP) and is estimated to be over $8,000 annually per person in the United States.

Mandated Health Insurance

Another principle that national health insurance tries to leverage is universal coverage. Those that are not yet sick and not concerned about health care in general are less likely to obtain health insurance. Typically, these are the young or those who cannot afford coverage. If this demographic is forced to buy health insurance, even though they are not using it, the premiums they pay help offset the premiums paid by those who are getting treatment. This is often framed as winners and losers. The "winners" are those who pay lower premiums because the risks are spread out more. The "losers" are those who have to pay for insurance they are not using.

One example of an Obamacare-type of mandated insurance coverage comes from Massachusetts: Romneycare.

Romneycare

The Massachusetts health care insurance reform law of 2006, informally (and ironically) known as Romneycare, requires Massachusetts residents to obtain health insurance. It mirrors Obamacare in some aspects, including government funding for those below a certain income level (set in Massachusetts at 150 percent of the poverty line). The act has undergone several modifications in the past six years to fit prevailing circumstances.

Some of the highlights include:

- Mandated insurance for all residents
- Tax penalties on employers with eleven or more full-time workers, who do not offer a qualifying plan
- A government body (Health Connector) that acts as a broker between private insurance and state residents
- Tax penalties for individuals who do not obtain insurance

After six years under this plan, some of the results are:

- Uninsured in Massachusetts dropped from 8 percent to 3 percent.
- Employment-based insurance increased from 70 percent to 76 percent, even though penalties are less than what premiums cost.
- Premiums for family policies have risen by 6.8 percent a year since 2007, although this is less than previous rate increases.
- About half of Massachusetts residents use the insurance exchange, but the half that do not have seen lower premiums in private plans due to competition with exchange-based insurers.
- Standardized plans through the exchange have limited choices for residents but lowered costs overall (compared to projections).
- Small businesses have been hurt the most, and many have dropped raises and bonuses to make up for the higher premiums they now pay.

Popularity among Massachusetts' residents varies, with poll outcomes highly dependent on how the question is asked. However, recent polls (2011 and 2012) show support running about 66 percent for and 33 percent against. In polls that show high dissatisfaction, there seems to be an overlap with complaints about health care in general instead of specifically about Romneycare. Someone who is displeased with their doctor, diagnosis, or treatment is more likely to respond unfavorably when surveyed. Specific complaints revolve around not being able to choose a physician or having to buy insurance when there seems to be no need.

APPRECIATING THE COMPLEXITIES

We've covered quite a bit—over one hundred years of health insurance—and have necessarily left a great deal out. But the overall picture is a movement toward third-party funding, either through employment or government entitlements, and a series of regulatory moves that changed how private insurance is administered.

One significant player we have left out is the individual state. Each state regulates the insurance sold within its borders, and adds regulations on the practice of medicine, including rules for doctors, hospitals, and pharmacies. Combined with the federal laws impacting health insurance, the result is a triumph of bureaucratic complexity. And this is the environment in which the ACA is meant to function.

Now that we've seen some of the major players and themes, the intent of the legislation will be clearer and the applications easier to spot. In the next chapter, Obamacare will be outlined to see how the current health insurance landscape shifts. Then, in Part II, individual circumstances will be covered.

CHAPTER 2

Obamacare Structure and Goals

In 1860, if you fell off your horse and hit your head, you may have taken the trouble to see a doctor, or you might have simply taken a half-day off with some ice on the bump. If you fall off your horse and hit your head today, you will be seen at a fully staffed emergency room, have X-rays or an MRI, get a neurological exam, pain medication, and advice on follow-up treatment. There will be dozens of professionals involved in your care, either directly or indirectly. We are also getting a great deal for the money, although the amount of money needed for this care is increasing at sometimes alarming rates.

THE RISING COST OF HEALTH CARE IN THE UNITED STATES

In the last two decades, life expectancy in the United States has risen from about seventy-five years to seventy-eight years. That's certainly due, at least in part, to better treatments for heart disease, cancer, and other illnesses. It wasn't that long ago that a diagnosis of malignant cancer was tantamount to a death sentence, but no longer. Innovation is part of the picture, and access to health care is another.

As a percentage of our national spending, the health care industry has grown to about 18 percent of the GDP. That means one out of every five dollars spent in the United States is used to purchase something related to health care. The trend lines have been clear for a long time. One of the few sectors of the economy immune to the recent Great Recession, health care employment and profits have remained robust (with a recent slowing from 2010 to 2013). Americans love their health care in the United States, and they pay a lot for it. As a percentage of GDP, the United States far exceeds other developed nations. The mantra seems to be, "Give us more and better health care and the heck with the price."

Government spending on health services has paralleled spending in the private sector, and reducing costs has been on the table politically for a long time. President Nixon's attempts to hold costs down and "Hillarycare" were discussed in the first chapter, and the forces pushing to address the problem have never gone away. From the conservative side of the aisle, it's a matter of reducing government spending by reining in costs. From the liberal side, lower costs mean more services can be had for those needing care. The result is bipartisan agreement on one fundamental fact: health care in the United States costs too much, and the trend is unsustainable.

WHY IS IT SO EXPENSIVE?

If other countries can have health services at a much cheaper rate than the United States, what are we doing wrong?

There is no easy answer to this question. Everyone concerned points to someone else as the culprit. Some of the main reasons given include (in no particular order):

- Doctors and other medical professionals are paid too much.
- Malpractice insurance and lawsuits artificially raise prices.
- New technology comes with increased costs.
- Pharmaceuticals are priced too high and drug companies use patent rights to make excessive profits.
- Inefficiencies in the health care system inflate costs.

- Oversight through government regulation is an expense that adds no value.
- Customized treatments lose economy of scale.
- An aging population increases costs because they use more services in their later years, and these services are more costly.
- Conditions are being treated with expensive health care that could best be prevented with lifestyle changes (particularly obesity).
- The rise in medical specialization over general practitioners pushes costs higher.
- A lack of real competition allows prices to soar.
- Tax benefits for health insurance and the third-party payer system inflate costs—people with insurance use more medical services because they don't pay directly, and they don't shop around.
- As a nation, we are unable to accept limits on health care based on price.

All of these drivers of health care costs were "on the table" when Obamacare was proposed. Some were removed as politically impossible. Almost all were modified from their original form. But the overarching goal remained the same: change the way the health care system functions and slow down the upward trend in costs.

THE PILLARS OF OBAMACARE

There are four main principles underlying the ACA. These represent the compromises reached in Congress. They address some of the problems above, but not all.

Lower Costs by Grouping Consumers

By accumulating small buyers of health services into larger groups, those groups can then negotiate for lower prices. This is the purpose of insurance exchanges: virtual marketplaces where qualified individuals and small businesses can combine buying power and buy insurance policies as a group.

Economies of scale also kick in so that insurance companies can save administration costs. Participating insurers also gain the power to negotiate lower prices with hospitals and other providers as they expand market share. An insurance exchange offers new customers to insurance companies—potentially thousands. Insurers are expected to help hold costs down if they wish to participate. Since insurance companies have the ability to set up networks and influence health care providers directly, this mechanism should act to keep overall expenses down.

Lower Premium Costs by Pooling Risk

Those who use more health care are more costly to insure. This is an unavoidable consequence of how insurance functions. Premiums paid by those who don't use the services go to cover costs from those who do. By mandating insurance for everyone, those who ordinarily would avoid buying coverage are now required to do so. These people become part of the risk pool. The effect is lower premiums overall.

To accomplish this pooled risk, everyone has to have access to affordable health insurance. This is where the employer mandate and insurance exchanges come in. By penalizing employers who do not offer health insurance, there is an incentive to make it available to their employees. Other ways to access insurance (exchanges and increased payments for low-income citizens) are mentioned below.

Focus on Preventive Care

Early detection and treatment can prevent more expensive conditions from developing. Other conditions can be avoided through lifestyle changes. Both of these save money for the health care system as a whole. Where there is scientific evidence that preventive care has a positive impact, Obamacare mandates that such services be offered.

Called *essential health benefits* (EHBs), many preventive services come with no co-pay or out-of-pocket costs and all have to be part of any qualifying insurance policy. Other benefits included under Obamacare make insurance policies meet basic requirements and allow consumers to choose between comparable coverage when shopping for insurance.

Reduce More Expensive Forms of Care

By mandating insurance across the population, the ACA makes it less likely that patients will seek treatment through emergency rooms for noncritical care. The overutilization of emergency rooms arose because current law keeps ERs from turning patients away. Those without insurance were more likely to get treatment at an ER and never pay the bill. They knew they couldn't be refused, and since they didn't have medical insurance, this was the primary way to get treatment. If no one is uninsured, there's no incentive to "beat the system."

Other types of expensive care are hit by Obamacare because insurance carriers push their policyholders toward less expensive forms of service. Network providers and hospitals negotiating contracts are meant to provide equivalent services at a lower cost. This is no different from other forms of buying in bulk. An insurance company that pre-buys one hundred MRIs, anticipating use by their members, will get a better deal.

OBJECTIONS TO OBAMACARE

While the principles previously outlined are laudable and economically sound, there are several real challenges. The first is whether the ends justify the means. Should the government have the ability to force someone to purchase a product they may not want? Is interference in a private industry (health insurance) warranted? This second question springs from the mandates on qualifying insurance policies. In effect, the government is telling insurance companies what they can and cannot sell to consumers.

One serious issue that has emerged is the battle between the federal government and state governments. While the federal government can penalize all citizens for not obtaining health insurance (the "stick" in Obamacare), they do not have the right to tell states how to run their own insurance or welfare programs. This is a real problem, since twenty-seven states have opted out of the insurance exchange program (as of September 2013). Residents in those states will use a federal insurance exchange instead.

Another big issue is how to get people who do not have insurance to buy it if they cannot afford the premiums. There's a segment of the population that is too well off to get Medicaid, but not well off enough to afford health insurance from a private carrier. To meet this problem, Medicaid has been expanded to people whose income is within 133 percent of the federal poverty line (FPL), and subsidies have been created to assist others whose income is within 400 percent of the FPL. Refusal to expand Medicaid in twenty-one states has effectively nullified this expansion for their low-income residents, leaving them ineligible for help from either Medicaid or the new federal insurance subsidies.

The Medicaid expansion and the insurance subsidies may become too much of a burden for the federal government to bear. In a time when financial default and the debt ceiling are political footballs, increased spending for what amounts to a social program is not only controversial but might be unsustainable. Some fear that, if expected savings do not emerge, Obamacare could bankrupt us. Others argue that the runaway costs of an unregulated system already distort the entire economy and if left unchecked could lead to even greater economic devastation.

In the end, Obamacare's greatest challenge is a political one. Resistance by state governments and opposition by politicians can delay implementation of Obamacare or force modifications.

There have been several delays of the rollout already, and some believe the entire act will be repealed before it gets established. If Obamacare works as intended, it will be a popular program—an outcome that would not go unnoticed in states that have resisted implementation, most of which border other states that would be enjoying the benefits. But if Obamacare is either killed politically or produces too many unwanted consequences, it will likely evaporate, as have previous attempts to stem the rising tide of health care costs.

PART II

Getting Started with the Affordable Care Act

CHAPTER 3

The Obamacare Timeline

The ACA promises health care security to the millions who fall between the cracks of for-profit insurance, nonprofit HMOs, current government health programs such as Medicare, and need-based public assistance. It sets standards for what it calls essential health benefits (EHBs) across all forms of assistance and insurance. It abolishes cost disparities between services for men and women, even as it recognizes that women have special health needs. And far-reaching as the ACA is meant to be in its effects, it is designed to be minimally disruptive to existing health care services and industries, and to the predominant provider of health insurance: employers. Moreover, individual states may establish, within limits, their own degrees of benefit and responsibility.

With all that complexity, it was necessary to implement various provisions of Obamacare over a period of years. This gradual implementation has been going on since the Patient Protection and Affordable Care Act, to use its full title, went into effect in 2010. This timeline overview focuses on provisions that directly affect patient protection regulation of the health care system and the insurance industry, and that seek to provide affordable care. Not noted here are provisions already or yet-to-be implemented that address supporting medical education and research; improving public health; reducing health care fraud, waste, economic disparities, and conflicts of interest; taxes and fees on certain profitable health care industries; and some temporary coverage programs designed to ease the transition to full implementation.

2010: The ACA expanded health coverage for young adults, for children, and for some others with preexisting conditions; outlawed insurance lifetime limits on benefits and other industry practices that denied or took away coverage; restricted annual benefit limits; abolished above-premium costs (co-pays) for immunizations and other recommended preventive health services; expanded tax credits for adoption; and established health plan appeal rights and assistance. The government also started providing tax credits for small business health plans (jump-starting a dramatic increase in covered employees even before maximum tax credits roll out in 2014). Various programs increased support for community health care clinics and services to rural and other underserved areas. Expansion of Medicaid was introduced as an opt-in program for individual states.

Need to Know:

- Most insurance industry regulations apply to new plans and policies.
- Existing plans and policies with old restrictions may be able to be replaced on full implementation of insurance market parity in 2014–2015.

2011: Medicare services were expanded or improved, including annual wellness visits, individualized preventive plans and services with no co-pay, and continued steps to remedy a structural flaw (the "donut hole") in the Medicare drug benefit. More Medicare dollars were directed to primary care physicians and general surgeons, and fewer to third-party Medicare Advantage (add-on services) providers. A Medicaid expansion supported homecare services for the disabled. Small businesses gained federal support for offering popular but expensive "cafeteria" (individual service choice) health plans for workers.

Insurance companies were required to justify any proposed rate increases and to account for how they spend the money they collect; that provision resulted in rate rebates to some policy holders. Several other provisions addressed cost control and uniformity of accounting across a range of health benefit plans.

Need to Know:

- The gap in Medicare's Part D drug benefit will be completely closed by 2020, after which benefits will rise evenly as drug costs rise.
- The disabled may have new options for home- and community-based care, rather than having to resort to state or other institutions.

2012: Twenty-two services focused on the special health needs of women were required to be included in all health insurance marketplace plans, and most other plans, at no above-premium cost (co-pay) to the patient. Employers were given a new option for offering long-term care plans through a voluntary payroll deduction. Insurers and health plans were required provide "a short, plain-language Summary of Benefits and Coverage" and uniform definitions of health care terms to enable honest comparison between plans.

Need to Know:

- Hospitals and nursing homes are subject to new federal monitoring and public reporting on the quality of their care.
- Federal payment changes will encourage individual physicians to form "accountable care organizations" for the purpose of standardized reporting of the quality of their care.

2013: A cornerstone of the ACA is the health insurance marketplaces, or "Marketplace," in federal shorthand, which are also known as health insurance exchanges or HIX. Data from implementation by participating states suggests that many rates for private health insurance will be lower than they have been. States also made their initial decisions about participating in expanded Medicaid coverage.

In order both to reap the benefits of the ACA and to avoid its penalties, the uninsured must enroll during the Marketplace Open Enrollment period that begins October 1, 2013 and ends March 31, 2014.

For most people, Marketplace implementation and its deadlines will overshadow other provisions that continue support for preventive services, administrative efficiency, cost reduction, better payments to doctors, and fees and limits designed to redistribute the total cost burden of health care.

Need to Know:

- Marketplace Open Enrollment begins October 1.
- Now is the time to gather the history of recent medical expenses and project upcoming needs.
- Check www.healthcare.gov for whether to enroll through a state or federal marketplace.
- The same Marketplace application will apply to both insurance and expanded Medicaid. The Marketplace may refer you to your state's application process, or will respond with either eligibility for Medicaid or the requirement to buy one of its insurance plans, along with information about any available subsidy.
- Small businesses—fewer than fifty full-time employee equivalents (FTEs)—may use the Small Business Health Options Program (SHOP) Exchange. Self-employed individuals use the individual marketplace.

2014: The first actual coverage through expanded Medicaid and the Marketplace begins January 1, 2014. Instant tax credits subsidize lower-income households' insurance costs. Preexisting condition exclusions, along with annual limits on EHBs and most cost differences based on individual circumstances, are abolished across all new plans and policies in all markets. Insurers may not end or restrict coverage for patients with life-threatening conditions who participate in clinical trials. The small business tax credit rises to one-half of employers' insurance cost. The range of health care providers required to report quality measures expands.

Need to Know:

- Some tax breaks require a "Silver" plan; what sounds like a limitation may have the effect of a subsidized upgrade.
- People with older individual policies that still exclude preexisting conditions or limit EHBs may be able to switch to Marketplace coverage to escape such restrictions.
- Smallest businesses (by size of payroll) get the largest tax credits.
- Open Enrollment ends March 31.
- Tax penalties for the uninsured begin at $95 per adult, half that amount for children. Individuals for whom no affordable plan is available are exempt from the penalty.

2015: Employer health benefit plans must meet standards for affordability and value essentially identical to (or better than) Marketplace plans. There is a simple, stringent comparison test. Businesses whose plans can't match or beat Marketplace plans pay a penalty tax designed to be more costly than providing compliant insurance. Businesses with fifty or more FTEs that do not offer health insurance also pay a penalty.

Medicare now pays physicians based on how well they treat their patients rather than on how many patients they treat. A new independent board addresses Medicare's solvency, evidence-based quality, patient access and outcomes, and cost-effectiveness.

Need to Know:

- In effect, all U.S. employers who offer health insurance must offer plans at least as valuable and as affordable as Marketplace plans, or pay comparable taxes for which neither they nor their employers receive direct benefits.
- Businesses with fifty or more FTEs that do not offer health insurance must pay a tax penalty for each employee after the first thirty.

2016–2018: The essential structures and mechanisms of the ACA are in place. Tweaks and expected ripple effects are detailed in the timeline below.

ACA TIMELINE

2013	• States establish health insurance marketplaces (aka Marketplace). • Marketplace Open Enrollment begins October 1.
2014	• Marketplace and expanded Medicaid coverage begins. • Preexisting condition exclusions are outlawed for any new insurance. • No new plans can set annual limits on EHBs. • Small business tax credits cover up to half of employer insurance costs. • Open Enrollment ends March 31.
2015	• Employers pay tax penalties for health plans that do not match or better Marketplace plans for affordability and value. • Businesses with fifty or more FTEs will pay tax penalties if they do not offer health insurance.
2016	• The individual (and family) tax penalties for not buying available insurance go from set to indexed amounts. • States may permit businesses with fifty to one hundred employees to buy insurance via SHOP.
2017	• States may permit larger businesses (over one hundred employees) to buy insurance via SHOP. • Virtually all "grandfathered" health plans—those exempt from the ACA insurance reforms—will have been abandoned by employers as no longer competitive.

2018 • A 40 percent excise ("luxury") tax is levied on insurance companies and plan administrators for annual insurance costs above $10,200 for self-only coverage and $27,500 for family plans. Over two years, these absolute-dollar "thresholds" become set by the Consumer Price Index. Insurers and employers are allowed higher thresholds for insuring higher-risk or higher-payout populations.

CHAPTER 4

The Individual Mandate

An early problem faced by legislators wanting to get all Americans on health insurance was how to reach those who resisted getting coverage. In some nations, universal health care is standard, and every citizen is automatically covered. But the idea of turning our health care system into a clone of Britain was dead on arrival in Congress. Ever since the Clinton administration, universal health care has been a dirty phrase, and there seemed to be no way forward if individual choice was kept in the mix.

ENTER THE INDIVIDUAL MANDATE

Those who don't want health insurance, even when it's free, make up an estimated seven million Americans. These are low-income families that qualify for Medicaid but simply don't sign up. How do we know about them? Other than estimates based on income, this group of the uninsured shows up at emergency rooms when they need treatment, and often they ignore the bills. Hospitals have been signing up patients for Medicaid on the spot, dedicating staff to gather the necessary information and submit the paperwork in the hopes of recovering some funds.

Two other groups weren't getting health insurance: those who couldn't afford it and those who felt they had no need for it. The first group fell into a gap where they made too much to qualify for Medicaid but not enough where they felt they could pay for their own health care. The second group was composed of younger, healthier adults who didn't interact with the health care system much. They felt health insurance wasn't worth paying for if they never, or only rarely, got sick.

Some people bridge two categories. For example, a typical college student can't afford to buy health insurance and is also healthy enough not to see a need. Obamacare addresses this group by allowing young adults (up to age twenty-six) to remain on a parent's policy as a dependent. This is not the same definition of dependent used to calculate taxes, and no other financial dependency has to exist (although it may).

The mandate is essentially a tax penalty. The penalty is paid on an individual basis and only happens if someone chooses not to get qualifying insurance. Doing this provides a financial motivation to get health insurance, even for those who do not want it.

Does it work? It has worked in Massachusetts, where participation in their early version of "Romneycare" went up to 97 percent after an individual mandate was imposed. The target for Obamacare is a bit lower; it will be considered to have achieved its objective if 94 percent of the population (not counting people residing in the United States without legal permission) is insured.

A PARALLEL WITH SOCIAL SECURITY

Social Security is a type of retirement insurance. You pay the "premiums" as a deduction from wages throughout your working career, and after retirement, the benefits are paid back. Obamacare could have worked this way as well, except that Social Security is a federal government–run program and a type of universal benefit all citizens enjoy. "Universal" and "federal government run" were the deal killers when it came to the ACA.

Obamacare is not funded (at least not mainly) by payroll taxes. But it still uses an important feature of how Social Security functions. To reach every citizen, Obamacare relies on Social Security numbers and federal tax filings. This is why the individual mandate will be enforced by the IRS as a tax penalty. There's really no other good way to connect health insurance to each citizen. Not all are employed, but all have Social Security numbers and pay taxes. Those who do not file taxes because of low income will now have to in order to avoid getting tagged with the individual mandate penalty.

If the individual mandate is the "stick," there are some carrots to spread around as well, and the final goal—getting health insurance for everyone—is still seen as worthy. But the mandate is a key motivator. There's nothing like a possible fine to push people into taking action.

WHY ARE SO MANY AMERICANS UNINSURED?

If health insurance were such a great deal, why are so many Americans without it? The number of citizens who are uninsured is about 50 million. (This number has fallen since Obamacare was enacted.) This doesn't count undocumented workers, which perhaps adds another 13 million.

About half of those currently insured get either Medicare or Medicaid. The other half are insured through employer-sponsored insurance plans. Medicare and Medicaid can be modified through legislation, but before Obamacare, those that got insurance through their workplace were at the mercy of a trend of lowered benefits, increased premiums, and employers dropping insurance benefits outright.

When people attempt to get health insurance outside of an employment-based group plan, they quickly find out just how expensive it can be. Without the leverage of a large pool of buyers, individuals are left paying the highest premiums for their age and health status. Many decide to buy health care only when needed, paying cash, or they use emergency rooms as a backup and take the financial hit. For some, any serious medical need that comes along will leave them bankrupt. Others never get treatment at all, allowing their medical conditions to worsen until a crisis is reached.

The simple explanation for why so many people are uninsured: it costs too much. And this is what the "affordable" in the Affordable Care Act is supposed to remedy.

HOW DOES THE INDIVIDUAL MANDATE CLOSE THE INSURANCE GAP?

First, the individual mandate incentivizes those who are eligible for fully or partially subsidized insurance to get signed up with Medicare or Medicaid. Second, it pushes those who are "insurance resistant" to get coverage. Those who cannot afford a policy are helped with subsidies. The ACA also has an employer mandate, making it more likely an employer will offer insurance to their workers. Finally, the ACA expands eligibility, allowing those who were just over the Medicaid-eligibility line (based on income) to get help.

If you are wondering what all this costs, so is everyone else. Budget estimates are funny things. No one really knows the true costs until a year or more after the books are closed. The mandate will directly help close the gap because those who do not get insurance will still be paying into the system— their penalties are based partly on their income, so that those who are doing better financially pay more.

But the primary way the individual mandate closes the insurance gap is by getting people to buy a policy. When doing so would cost more than about one-tenth of the household income, subsidies are offered to help pay the price. Still, forcing someone to buy insurance isn't popular with many— it reeks of government intrusion into what should be an individual choice. Some feel that taking the risk to go without insurance is tied to individual freedom. Still others criticize the individual mandate as an overreach of authority by the federal government. This last objection was the subject of a U.S. Supreme Court challenge.

THE SUPREME COURT RULES ON THE INDIVIDUAL MANDATE

The first version of the ACA had a state mandate. The mandate would have removed all federal funding for Medicaid if states didn't match funds and expand Medicaid to cover more of the low-income uninsured. The states were successful in overturning this aspect, and Medicaid expansions will be paid for with federal dollars instead. However, in a controversial ruling, the individual mandate survived the challenge.

The point of law was whether or not the federal government could use the commerce clause in the Constitution to levy a tax. It turns out they couldn't, but they could still tax someone for something they didn't do. Chief Justice John Roberts wrote the deciding opinion, saying:

> The individual mandate cannot be upheld as an exercise of Congress's power under the Commerce Clause. That clause authorizes Congress to regulate interstate commerce, not to order individuals to engage in it. In this case, however, it is reasonable to construe what Congress has done as increasing taxes on those who have a certain amount of income, but choose to go without health insurance. Such legislation is within Congress's power to tax.

The states did win some important concessions though, in that much more of the funding for Obamacare comes from federal coffers than was originally intended.

WHAT DOES OBAMACARE MEAN FOR U.S. TAXPAYERS?

If you obtain health insurance and avoid the tax penalties, you will still have to prove you did so. Reporting requirements kick in for 2014, and although the IRS hasn't yet shared the details, your health insurance status will be reported on your W-2 form (if you get insurance through your employer). Those who purchase private insurance, and those who get Medicaid or Medicare, will have a form submitted to the IRS, identifying the type of policy, who it covers (family members), and the Social Security number of the policyholder. This is similar to the 1099 form used for miscellaneous income.

If you do owe a penalty, the IRS will treat it like any other tax debt. If you have a refund coming, it will be reduced by the amount of the penalty, and if that doesn't cover it, you will be billed by the IRS. The statute makes it clear that not paying the penalty isn't a crime—at least not something you'll go to jail for. But the IRS can continue to try to collect from you until it's paid. Anyone who's been hounded by the IRS knows how effective this can be.

Penalties owed accrue from year to year, and you won't get a refund on a penalty if you do buy a policy after the fact. One stipulation to note is a three-month forbearance. Because it may take time to get a policy in place—either because you've changed jobs or lost your insurance for another reason—taxpayers are not penalized for a gap in coverage of up to three continuous months. Those who want to protest the individual mandate without paying the penalty could simply cancel their policy for three months and keep the premiums, as long as they got insurance right afterward.

The penalties start in 2014 at $95 or 1 percent of your income (whichever is larger), up to a maximum of $285. (The maximum penalty is always three times the minimum.) In 2015, this jumps up to $325 and $975. In 2016, it goes to $695 and $2,085. If you see a trend there, you are correct—the stick gets bigger the longer you hold out, increasing the financial pain. After 2016, the penalties are calculated on cost-of-living increases.

OTHER TAXES

Taxes also increase on a variety of items:

- Capital gains taxes go up by 3.8 percent on single income above $200,000 and household income above $250,000. Designed to tap into the more affluent Americans, this can also hit homeowners who sell their property at a large profit. This took effect on January 1, 2013.

- Medicare taxes go up for single income above $200,000 and household income above $250,000, from 1.45 percent to 2.35 percent.
- New taxes are levied on medical devices and tanning salons.
- An excise tax is imposed on high-value health care plans, usually offered to top executives (Cadillac plans).

Although not a tax, drug companies will be paying into the system by giving a 50 percent discount to Medicare patients who otherwise would have to pay out-of-pocket for prescriptions (the so-called donut hole, which is explained in detail in chapter 13.)

With the new taxes and the possibility of a penalty, the individual mandate accomplishes one of its goals: it gets the attention of those Obamacare is trying to reach. It will no longer be possible to ignore health insurance in the United States. One way or another, health insurance will matter much more than it has before.

CHAPTER 5

Health Insurance Exchanges

To meet the "affordable" description in the ACA, a way had to be found to offer health insurance at a rate most Americans could pay without breaking their budgets. At the extremes—the lowest and highest incomes—this wasn't a problem. Medicaid has been offered to the poor for decades, and seniors are eligible for Medicare. Citizens with high incomes were already able to buy good health insurance, and those with good jobs usually had health insurance available through their employers. But this still left a sizeable chunk of the population without coverage.

One way the ACA attempts to bridge this insurance gap is through health insurance exchanges (HIXs) and government-based subsidies to make insurance affordable. An HIX is a virtual marketplace where standardized insurance policies from private companies are offered to the public. In fact, as the federal government implemented an online gateway to the state exchanges and its own exchange for citizens of non-participating states, it adopted the blanket term *Marketplace* to describe the HIXs in the aggregate. We use the terms interchangeably: most often *HIX* in general discussions and *Marketplace* when referring to the nuts and bolts of individual participation. A separate exchange—the Small Business Health Options Program (SHOP)—is offered to small businesses so they can buy insurance for their employees.

WHY DOES THE UNITED STATES NEED HEALTH INSURANCE EXCHANGES?

If a universal, government-run, tax-funded health insurance system had been adopted, there would be no need for exchanges. But universal health care was neither politically feasible nor economically possible when the ACA was enacted. Even the exchanges themselves faced problems—there was the constitutional question of whether or not the federal government could regulate insurance companies at all, since insurance is regulated at the state level. The result of these political and legal battles is a system that has the same general goal across the nation but varies in implementation state by state.

The problem that insurance exchanges try to fix is an economic one. Small groups (or individuals) who purchase health insurance on their own are charged as much as 18 percent more than larger groups, even when the coverage offered is equivalent. Economies of scale are one reason—smaller groups cost more to administer on a per patient basis—but also because small groups don't have the buying power to negotiate better terms.

With potentially thousands of new customers shopping at an HIX, insurance companies have an incentive to get on board and provide insurance under the guidelines established. Individuals have an incentive to use them because they can shop for policies online, easily compare different products, and in many cases, get a subsidy (based on income) to help pay premium costs.

UNDERSTANDING ACTUARIAL VALUE

The insurance plans offered through an HIX are ranked by actuarial value, a concept that allows comparisons between policies, even when those policies are very complex. The actuarial value is based on a statistical average of what policyholders pay into the plan versus what they collect in benefits.

At the root of all insurance systems is a very simple idea: get a bunch of people to put money into a pot and then redistribute the money to those who need it. The insurance company acts as the caretaker and accountant, but essentially, all insurance does is take money from one set of policyholders and give it to another. How do they know how much to take in as premiums so they don't run out of money? That's where the average comes in. No one can predict exactly how much any one person will need to cover their health care costs. Instead, they total up all the money spent and divide it by how many people are in the risk pool. That tells you how much to collect in premiums.

The average person here isn't male or female, black or white, young or old—all that matters is how much money that person draws out, balanced with how much they pay in. This fictitious average person will pay exactly the same amount in premiums as they get in benefits.

In practice, some people will use more services than others. Those who fall ill will get more in benefits than those who stay healthy. But everyone pays the same in premiums based on averages of the overall costs.

In the HIX model, policies are ranked by how much the policy covers for the average person getting the average level of treatment over a year. If the policy has an actuarial value of 60 percent, that means the average policyholder will pay 40 percent of the costs of their care over a year, with the insurance policy covering the remaining 60 percent. It's also important to note that this 60 percent will determine the premium price. (Remember, all the money comes from policyholders; it's just redistributed.)

Although this simple model is correct, insurance companies do much more than move money around. They not only administer the policies but negotiate for better prices with providers, set up networks, and bargain with drug suppliers. They are also involved in treatment standards and certifications of doctors and hospitals.

The higher the actuarial value of a policy, the more it covers when health care is used, but the trade-off is a higher premium. The entire purpose of setting different actuarial values is to allow consumers to shop intelligently. By comparing policies with the same actuarial value, you can be assured you are comparing apples to apples.

WHAT WILL AN HIX OFFER?

Health insurance exchanges will have at least one Platinum or Gold policy, and at least one Silver or Bronze policy (other policies will be mentioned later). They may have all four, but they have to have at least one of the top two and one of the bottom two.

Actuarial values are set under this system as:

- Platinum: 90 percent
- Gold: 80 percent
- Silver: 70 percent
- Bronze: 60 percent

Premiums will go up to reflect the higher values and, remember, the percentages listed are the amount a policy is expected to cover for an average person in the plan who uses an average level of health care over a year.

This doesn't mean all plans will be the same. By switching benefits around, one plan—even with the same color code—may be better for an individual than another. For example, if you and your partner are anticipating starting a family, maternity care benefits will be of greater interest to you than services aimed at the aging. Vision and dental services will also differentiate plans, and some networks will be more appealing based on location and whether or not the patient's current doctor participates.

Two other policy types may be offered through an HIX. The first is a catastrophic policy with limited benefits and a reduced premium. This will be available only to those under thirty years of age or those who obtain a hardship exemption (uncommon), and is meant to be a "bare bones" policy—just enough to meet the individual mandate and avoid a tax penalty. A second type called the "Basic Health Plan" may be offered by states (it is not mandatory) for low-income participants. This plan will mimic the bronze level of coverage for those with incomes between 133 percent and 200 percent of the poverty level.

For those between 133 percent and 400 percent of the federal poverty line (FPL), subsidies will be offered to help pay premium costs through the exchange. These are also on a sliding scale, with actual amounts posted by the Department of Health and Human Services (HHS).

How an Exchange Works

The incentive for participation by an insurance company is access to customers. A tremendous new influx of potential customers will be created by the individual mandate, and many of those will seek health insurance through an HIX. Opening this new market gives the government a way to influence private insurance companies by setting restrictions on what kind of policies will be offered.

Other than the color-coded rankings mentioned earlier, policies must meet several other criteria:

- **Lower out-of-pocket limits:** The dollar amount policyholders must meet before the insurance pays 100 percent of costs will be lower. The maximum out-of-pocket amount is determined by the limits set on health savings accounts (HSAs) (adjusted yearly). Those who make less than 400 percent of the FPL get an even lower limit.
- **Lower premiums:** Subsidies will be provided for individuals with incomes up to 400 percent of the FPL, on a sliding scale. Even those at the top will not have to pay more than 9.5 percent of their income for premiums. Those closer to the 133 percent "floor" (based on expanded Medicaid availability) will not pay more than 2 percent of their income in premiums.

- **All policies must cover preventive care:** This suite of benefits is set by the HHS, and policyholders will not pay fees for these services (no out-of-pocket deductible or co-pay).
- **All policies (except catastrophic plans) will cover essential health benefits (EHBs):** EHBs are a set of service categories (mental health, addiction treatment, prescription drugs, laboratory, and other services). Exactly what is covered in each category is still to be determined and will reflect what employer insurance policies in a particular state are offering.
- **All policies must perform well:** Those that consistently underperform will be dropped from the HIX.

States may either participate by setting up their own HIX, or partner with the federal government to do so, or even combine with other states to make a regional HIX. States can also opt out of the process entirely. In the latter case, the federal government will step in and run the HIX, based on current state-level insurance regulations.

An HIX for Small Businesses

A separate but parallel health exchange will be set up for small businesses that wish to offer health insurance to their employees. "Small" in this context means fewer than one hundred employees. Very small businesses (less than twenty-five employees) can receive tax credits for using the system, depending on how much the business contributes to the premium costs for their workers.

Called the Small Business Health Options Program (SHOP) Exchange, the purpose is to allow small businesses access to competitive plans with set benefits. SHOP is an attempt to level the playing field between small and large companies, since large companies, based solely on the number of employees, have more leverage when it comes to negotiating lower rates.

By 2017, large businesses may be offered access to SHOP. By then, their competitive advantage is expected to have disappeared as large-company health insurance policies move closer to the offerings on exchanges. Businesses that start out on the SHOP exchange at fewer than one hundred employees, but later grow to more than one hundred, will still be allowed to participate.

Emerging Problems

While insurance companies have an incentive to participate, it turns out individual states may not. As of September 2013, with a deadline for action of October 2013, only sixteen states (plus the District of Columbia) have authorized state-level insurance exchanges. Seven more have decided on a hybrid type where states partner with the federal government to run an HIX. These hybrids may transition to a state-only HIX later. But that leaves twenty-seven states that are not going to participate.

For states that aren't setting up a state-run exchange, the ACA allows a federal HIX as the default. While this seems like a practical solution, it may be very difficult to implement, if only because the expertise in state-level insurance law resides with each state. It isn't possible to make a cookie-cutter exchange that will fit each of the states that have opted out. No one is sure the federal government will be able to pull it off.

Another hurdle to overcome involves coordinating all the details. HIXs are supposed to offer online access with ease of use—meaning consumers can shop and buy policies quickly and with full transparency. But this all has to be set up, including getting policies approved and subsidies in place, and presenting it in a format the public can understand. With millions of potential customers, it's no small task to get all the pieces in place, and states have been delaying implementation, either because of political battles, funding issues, or the normal bureaucratic slow-shuffle.

If the exchanges don't start up in 2014, Obamacare risks being judged unworkable. Some elements have already been delayed, but holding back on HIXs would preempt other parts of the program, too. In particular, the SHOP exchanges are tied to the employer mandate (which has been delayed until 2015 already), and the regular HIXs are needed so that low-income earners can access subsidized policies. Without HIXs, it's unrealistic to impose the individual mandate, since the exchanges are the default place to buy a qualifying policy.

CHAPTER 6

Meeting Your Mandate in the Marketplace

Most people have at one time or another had to choose a health insurance plan—whether from options provided by an employer or in the general private insurance market. Typically this involves using a worksheet to project one's health care needs and compare them to the options offered by particular health plans, weighing such items as types and extent of coverage (including for preexisting conditions and other special needs), premium cost, out-of-pocket expenses (co-pays and deductibles), whether co-pays count against deductibles, and so on. Under the ACA, this process changes in significant ways:

- Many aspects of coverage comparison have become moot, because the ACA mandates what it calls essential health benefits (EHBs), including preventive services that must be offered free of out-of-pocket cost.
- Preexisting conditions are no longer an issue.
- Premium costs are more closely competitive and easier to compare. The traditional inverse relationship between premium costs and out-of-pocket expense has been stratified into Platinum (highest premium, lowest deductible), Gold, Silver, and Bronze (lowest premium, highest deductible) plans.

The "homework" required before venturing into the Marketplace also differs. It is still necessary, of course, to know what past medical expenses have been and to project whether they might rise, fall, or stay constant in the future. However, exploring options in the Marketplace (and for expanded Medicaid, where available) may require additional information. For example, at www.healthcare.gov, to generate the most informative list of options and an individual checklist of items required for application, an individual would need to supply information about:

- State of residence (after which you may be referred to your state's website for enrollment)
- Sex
- Age range
- Insurance status (e.g., preexisting insurance, or whether employers' health insurance coverage is available to household members, whether or not they are using it)
- Household size
- Number of dependents or other personal information that might affect particular kinds of eligibility
- General income level

Small business owners will be asked:

- State of operation
- Number of full-time equivalent employees (FTEs)
- Whether they currently offer health insurance

This information is anonymous and confidential, and does not affect the actual application process. While it is not necessary to provide this information to get the full range of information available at www.healthcare.gov, doing so may make the process easier.

If your state is implementing its own active participation in the ACA, it will also have published information about how to participate and benefit, and the options available to you. Check your state's website, where information for participating states will probably be featured prominently, and/or available via the state's Department of Public Health or

Insurance Commission. The site www.healthcare.gov will also refer you to your state's screening and enrollment website if it has one.

Another valuable source of information for individuals and families is the Henry J. Kaiser Family Foundation, which offers an interactive online calculator to help you estimate where your circumstances place you in the Marketplace, including eligibility for Medicaid or premium subsidies. Please note that the Kaiser Family Foundation calculator (http://kff.org/interactive/subsidy-calculator) does not take into account variations due to your state of residence. You may find its information most useful in conjunction with the information from www.healthcare.gov or your participating state's website.

What Obamacare Means for You

CHAPTER 7

Frequently Asked Questions

Is the Affordable Care Act (ACA) the same thing as Obamacare?

In common usage, yes. Technically, the ACA is just the legislation (the Patient Protection and Affordable Care Act) and the amendments to it. Obamacare is broader and includes all the rulings and agency regulations that flow from the act. For example, the ACA might create and authorize an agency to oversee some aspects of the law, and the rules the agency imposes aren't in the act itself. But those new rules would be part of Obamacare. In this book, we use the terms interchangeably.

What does "affordable" mean in the Affordable Care Act?

Ideally, you should be spending no more than 9.5 percent of your income to pay for health care, including coverage and out-of-pocket costs. If you have a low income, the percentage is even less. Both penalties and subsidies are designed to keep that percentage stable.

What is the individual mandate?

It's a penalty imposed by the Internal Revenue Service (IRS) on those who do not obtain (either directly or through an employer) a qualifying health insurance policy. The "employer mandate" is similar, but the tax penalties are directed at businesses instead.

What if I don't have insurance? Will I have to pay?

Starting in the 2014 tax year, if you do not obtain insurance, you will be penalized. The penalties are calculated partially on your income, and they increase each year. In the first year, you will owe either $95 or up to 1 percent of your income, whichever is greater. The penalty maxes out at $285 for 2014, but jumps higher every year thereafter.

Can't I get an exemption?
Unlikely. There are a few select groups that are exempt from Obamacare, but these groups either offer their own insurance or do not participate in other social programs. For example, some Amish communities do not participate in Social Security or Medicare, and they are exempt from Obamacare. People residing in the United States without legal permission are also exempt, but immigration reform may change this.

I am a sole proprietor / I own my own business. Will I have to get insurance?
Yes. The individual mandate does not discriminate—everyone will have to get coverage or pay a tax penalty. To offset this, those with lower incomes may qualify for a subsidy. Your status as a business owner does not exempt you from the mandate.

How will the government know if I have health insurance?
The IRS is responsible for imposing the penalties for the individual mandate. Employers and others will report your status with your Social Security number in much the same way your wages are reported. Those who are unemployed still have Social Security numbers and are still required to have health insurance.

What if I can't afford to get a policy on my own?
Depending on your income level, you may be eligible for a subsidy or even full coverage at government expense. Provisions are in place to offer discounts to anyone whose income is up to 400 percent of the federal poverty line (FPL). Currently (2013), for an individual, the poverty line is set at $11,490 (for a family of four, it's $23,550). Some type of subsidy is available for people whose income is up to four times those amounts, and those amounts are adjusted yearly.

Where can I find out what the current FPL is?

The Department of Health and Human Services (HHS) publishes the guidelines. You can find the most up-to-date listing on their website: http://aspe.hhs.gov/poverty/index.cfm.

I think I'm eligible for a subsidy; how can I find out the amount?

Several subsidy calculators have been published online. These allow you to enter some basic information about your family income and generate a reasonable estimate. One can be found at http://kff.org/interactive/subsidy-calculator. You may wish to use more than one calculator to double-check, and the final arbiter of your subsidy will be the insurance exchange itself.

Will I be able to get cheap insurance?

This depends on your age, employment situation, and income. Those who are over the age of sixty-five qualify for Medicare. Those under 133 percent of the poverty level qualify for Medicaid, if their state of residence participates. Others will be offered insurance through an employer or a family member. Finally, those left over will be able to buy insurance through an insurance exchange. Whether the insurance premiums and benefits are "cheap" depends on your income, where you get your insurance, and how much you use the health care system. In general, the more care you receive, the more you will pay.

When do I have to have a policy by?

Insurance exchanges will be offering open enrollment from October 2013 through March 2014. If you will be using an exchange (and if those dates do not change), you will need to get a policy during that time period. Those who get insurance through an employer may have other open enrollment dates. In all cases, you have a three-month grace period before the penalty kicks in, and the clock starts ticking on January 1, 2014.

Will I have to switch doctors?

This depends entirely on which insurance policy you purchase. It works the same way as a change in insurance: when an insurer has a contract relationship with doctors or hospitals, you will be directed to those in their network. Obamacare doesn't change this directly, but it is expected that insurers will compete for business by expanding their networks and striving to obtain the lowest possible costs for services. In some cases, it will mean a doctor switch, but this isn't due to Obamacare; it's because doctors may decide not to participate in a particular network of providers.

Will I get freebies under Obamacare?

Yes and no. Every benefit offered by an insurance policy is paid for by someone. Those who benefit most get subsidized policies, either through government funding or partial payment by an employer. Others will pay regular premium levels and see several free services, at least free at the point of care. In reality, the free services are paid for by premiums when purchasing a policy. The only difference is that some essential preventive care is rendered with no out-of-pocket costs (no fees, no deductible, and no co-pay). These benefits are built into every qualified policy. There are other minimum requirements, but those benefits may include a co-pay or a deductable.

Will essential health benefits (EBHs) be free?

No. Although policies will have to include care in several areas, these EBHs can have co-pays or deductibles. Exactly what is covered as an EHB is yet to be determined by the HHS and may vary in detail by state. There is a subset of preventive care benefits that are free, but not all EHBs fall into this category.

My state opted out of Obamacare. What does that mean for me?

States can opt out of only two areas of the law. The first is whether or not a state chooses to set up an insurance exchange. Twenty-seven states have decided not to. The federal government has set up an exchange to cover citizens of those states. Not much changes from the consumer's standpoint.

The second opt-out is whether or not states accept federal money to expand Medicaid in their state (up to 133 percent of the FPL). A Supreme Court decision allows states to refuse to expand Medicaid. Opposition to expanding Medicaid has not been softened by the federal government's offer of more generous subsidies, leaving about two out of three people intended to be covered by the expansion with no new health insurance options. In a painful irony, they are too poor to receive Marketplace subsidies, and not poor enough to qualify for Medicaid under the old guidelines.

Those who are uncertain about their Medicaid status should apply anyway, through their states or through the Marketplace. The number of people who currently qualify for Medicaid under the old rules is unknown. The existing rules are complicated as well as varied, and parents who do not qualify, for example, may have children who do. Since Marketplace eligibility screening is based on whole-household information, some who have fallen through the cracks of their state's system may still be able to get some minimal coverage.

The other provisions of Obamacare are directed at employers, individuals, health care providers, and insurance companies. State participation is not required.

Which states have opted out of a state-run insurance exchange?
As of May 2013, the following states have decided not to operate their own insurance exchanges:

Alabama, Alaska, Arizona, Florida, Georgia, Indiana, Kansas, Louisiana, Maine, Mississippi, Missouri, Montana, Nebraska, New Jersey, North Carolina, North Dakota, Ohio, Oklahoma, Pennsylvania, South Carolina, South Dakota, Tennessee, Texas, Utah, Virginia, Wisconsin, and Wyoming.

If my state opted out, does that mean I don't have to participate in Obamacare?
No. You are still required to obtain insurance. Opting out of a state-run or federal-state partnership insurance exchange means that you will have access (if you qualify) to an exchange run by the federal government instead.

How will I find out the details for my state?

As of October 1, 2013, you can do a general online search, check the federal government's health care website (www.healthcare.gov), or look for information through your state's health department website. If you are in a nonparticipating state, the information will be available at www. healthcare.gov.

How will I participate if I am unable to go online?

For ease of use, Obamacare insurance exchanges (both state and federal) are designed to be accessed over the Internet. If you are unable to use the Internet, unfamiliar with computers, or uncertain about the process, you can access the same information through your state or county health department. You should call and find out what procedures they have in place. You may be referred to a public or private agency that has received special training in assisting consumers who need help with the process.

Will my premiums rise under Obamacare?

That depends on your policy. Policies that meet the minimum requirements to qualify under Obamacare will rise the least. Discounted policies that do not offer enough coverage will rise the most. Most will go up because of new rules preventing high deductibles, limits on payouts, and not allowing rejection for preexisting conditions. The increases are expected to level off and even fall as more people get policies that otherwise wouldn't. However, while adding healthy people to the risk pool should hold premiums down, no one really knows if this will make up for the increases already seen.

Premiums will fall for those who are now qualified to get subsidies based on income. They may also fall for those who get insurance through a small business (a business with fewer than one hundred employees), since an insurance exchange will open up specifically for small business use, with discounts available.

In general, the cost of health care in the United States has trended upward for decades. Obamacare is meant to slow this trend, not reverse it. The challenge from critics is whether or not this is accomplished by the ACA.

How can I find out if my current health insurance meets the qualifications under Obamacare?

There is no set method. Currently, the best way is to ask your insurer. Eventually, only qualified plans will be in play, as grandfathered plans disappear and insurers meet the new minimum standards.

Do VA benefits (TRICARE) qualify under Obamacare?

TRICARE insurance meets the Obamacare qualifications, and veterans under that system will not have to change insurance. Veterans' health benefits other than TRICARE may or may not satisfy the requirement; check at www.healthcare.gov or with the Department of Veterans Affairs.

I have a high-deductible plan. Will I need to change insurance?

Maybe. Under Obamacare, only single persons under thirty years of age are allowed to meet the individual mandate with a "catastrophic" type of policy, which includes a high-deductible, lower premiums, and limited coverage.

What is a Cadillac plan?

Some policies are offered with extremely high benefits and premiums. These may have been negotiated as part of a compensation package (usually for union members or company executives). Starting in 2018 (unless this changes), those policies with yearly premiums higher than $10,200 for an individual ($27,500 for a family) will pay a penalty. The penalty is a tax imposed on the insurance company, amounting to 40 percent of the premium costs above these ceiling amounts.

What if I want to purchase more coverage than the basic plans offered?

You only need a qualifying plan to meet the requirements of the individual mandate, but you may purchase other coverage, if you wish. For example, dental and vision coverage are common add-ons. These can be purchased as either riders on a policy or as separate insurance.

What is the Medicaid eligibility gap?

Obamacare sets subsidy eligibility for purchasing insurance on an exchange at 133 percent of the FPL. The assumption was that people or families making less than this would be eligible for Medicaid and would not need to buy private health insurance. But in the wake of a Supreme Court decision striking down mandatory state compliance, about half the states have refused outright the federal plan to expand Medicaid eligibility—along with drastically increased federal funding—or are still debating participation.

Non-participating states typically set Medicaid eligibility at 100 percent of the FPL, or even lower. This leaves a "Medicaid gap" in which millions of people—about two out of three intended to be covered by Medicaid expansion—have hardly any better recourse for health care than they had before: primarily emergency room care that is both costly and inappropriate for many chronic and life-threatening conditions.

CHAPTER 8

Insurance for Adult Females

The majority of the health care changes that adult women will see under the ACA come through a shift in standardized coverage. Policies will have to meet certain minimum requirements, many of which are directed specifically at women's health care issues.

ALL ADULT WOMEN

Obamacare attempts to remove insurance price differences between the genders while still recognizing the special services females need. For example, insurers will no longer be allowed to charge a higher premium for an insurance policy based on gender.

Beginning in 2014, new insurance plans must stop doing "gender rating" when determining premiums. This technique has been used to offer lower-cost insurance to males—a group that uses fewer services overall and which received a discount because of it. This same provision takes effect for federally sponsored health care insurance as well.

According to the Department of Health and Human Services, preventive and supportive services without any shared costs (no deductible or co-pay) have been scientifically shown to lower overall health care costs. The idea is to catch problems early to either prevent them altogether or treat them before they get worse. Screening and counseling are the main methods used.

Grandfathered plans (even when an out-of-network provider is used) have to meet these standards.

One newsworthy Obamacare provision was the cancellation of co-pays for birth control. This change went into effect in July 2012.

PREVENTIVE SERVICES FOR ADULT WOMEN

- **Well-woman visits** are covered as an annual benefit. The specific services covered will depend on age and status. For example, a woman of childbearing age will be offered preconception care (counseling, vitamins, birth-control advice), while a woman postmenopause will not. Older women may receive counseling about bone health (calcium uptake) and younger women might not. Breast exams and mammograms are offered based on current guidelines.

  Although the well-woman visit is set as an annual event meant to give women direct contact with preventive-care services, the guidelines note that multiple visits might be required, depending on the tests and screenings conducted. Where multiple appointments are needed, these are also covered in full.

- **Gestational diabetes screening** is provided as part of the first prenatal visit and again at six months (and more often for those who fall under a high-risk category because of weight, history, or other factors). Pregnancy services also include anemia testing, bacteriuria testing, chlamydial infection screening, Rh incompatibility screening, and others.

- **Breastfeeding support**, along with supplies and training, will be offered to pregnant women who request the service. Equipment needed for breastfeeding, such as pumps, are covered.

- **Domestic violence** counseling is covered, regardless of marital status. Screening is also covered, although this may only consist of a questionnaire. Screening is recommended regardless of whether or not a woman shows signs of abuse.

- **HPV testing** is covered for women starting at thirty years of age. Human papillomavirus is considered a risk factor for developing some types of cervical cancer. Repeat testing is recommended every three years. This testing is not connected to sexual activity, since the virus can be transmitted in other ways.
- **STD counseling** is covered for all sexually active women. Sexually transmitted disease counseling is covered annually and will probably be rolled into a well-woman visit. Testing for chlamydia, syphilis, and other STDs are covered. Some tests are based on risk factors or as part of pregnancy services.
- **HIV counseling** and screening is covered for sexually active women. Although HIV is not specifically a sexually transmitted infection, the ACA treats it as such for purposes of benefit payments.
- **Contraception** counseling and prescriptions for birth control are covered for women of childbearing age. There has been some political fallout because of this provision and some religious-based organizations are exempt. As of July 2013, challenges to Obamacare's requirements on contraception were still being raised as freedom of religion issues under the Constitution.

Effective August 1, 2013, a religious employer is defined as an employer that is organized and operates as a nonprofit entity and is referred to in section 6033(a)(3)(A)(i) or (iii) of the Internal Revenue Code. Such an employer is exempt from the provisions on contraception.

THE U.S. PREVENTIVE SERVICES TASK FORCE

The U.S. Preventive Services Task Force (USPSTF) is a government agency tasked with determining what preventive medical services have a strong, or "high certainty," of either a substantial (grade A) or moderate (grade B) benefit. There are lower ratings, but services with an A or B rating have to be covered at no cost. For women, there are several screening/care items of note recommended:

- **Aspirin** to prevent cardiovascular disease (fifty-five to seventy-nine years of age)
- **Folic acid** supplements for all women of childbearing age
- **Breast cancer screening**, including presenting options, with a mammogram every one or two years for women over forty
- **BRCA screening** for women with a family history of breast cancer. BRCA is a genetic variant that predisposes women to breast cancer
- **Cervical cancer screening** (Pap smear) every three years for women aged twenty-one to sixty-five. This interval between exams can be extended to every five years when cytology is done and a patient is HPV negative
- **Cholesterol screening** for women over twenty when there is an increased risk of coronary artery disease (based on lifestyle, obesity, and other considerations)
- **Osteoporosis screening** for women sixty-five or older, or for younger women at increased risk

There are other tests and services offered, but these are specific to females. It is assumed that most will be done as a suite during annual well-woman visits. Pregnant women are eligible for other screening and counseling services related to prenatal care. The preceding list does not include screenings available to all adults (such as high blood pressure checks).

MATERNITY CARE AND PREEXISTING CONDITIONS

One of the "fixes" in the Obamacare mix is coverage for maternity care. Maternity care will have to be a benefit under all policies offered. Estimates are that only about 12 percent of insurance policies included this feature previously. This was partially due to who was purchasing the insurance, since discounts could be offered to men or women past their childbearing years.

A related issue is coverage for preexisting conditions. A rather embarrassing characteristic of the private health insurance marketplace was treating gender as a preexisting condition. The strange logic of it was that being female meant someone would use more health care services and should pay a higher premium. This practice has now been done away with.

For females who have had a cesarean section, or who have been the victim of spousal abuse, these preexisting conditions can no longer be used to deny coverage. The same is true for someone who seeks health care who is already pregnant (the pregnancy is a preexisting condition).

Those who were uninsured and have a preexisting condition can obtain temporary insurance through what is known as a "preexisting condition insurance plan." These plans are meant to fill the gap before "normal" coverage takes effect.

WHAT ABOUT ABORTION?

There is no equivalent to abortion when it comes to contentious debate in women's health care. Currently, federal funds may not be used to provide abortion services (which include emergency contraception, the so-called "morning-after pill") under what is known as the Hyde Amendment, a law that has been renewed on a yearly basis by Congress. The law does have an exception for pregnancies that result from rape, incest, or that threaten the life of the mother.

Because of the Hyde Amendment, Obamacare cannot mandate coverage of abortion services. Instead, coverage is handled on the state level, with some states paying for abortions under state-funded Medicaid and other states declining to do so. Under Obamacare, this situation will not change.

CHAPTER 9

Insurance for Adult Males

While many of the new rules under Obamacare pick out subgroups of the population for particular attention—offering new services and low or no co-pays—adult men fall into a default group. Since insurance benefits are balanced against costs, with a benefit added in one area raising costs in another, the historical health care insurance bargain enjoyed by adult men, on the whole, suffers.

Overall, premiums for adult men are expected to rise, and as a demographic, healthy men will pay more than they do now to help finance other groups. The reason isn't simply because the ACA sets out to place more costs on men—that is not part of the legislation. Rather, men as a group started with a better deal—a "deal" they will mostly lose.

INSURANCE FOR MEN BEFORE AND AFTER THE ACA

One of the ways insurance companies can be competitive is to offer lower premiums to groups that don't use as many services. By gathering statistics on health care utilization, an insurer can target specific groups that have a lower risk. We are most familiar with this in other forms of insurance. For instance, if you live in a fireproof house, you should pay less for fire insurance, or if your car has excellent safety ratings, you might pay a lower premium, as well.

A study from the University of California, published in 2000, put it this way:

> Women had a significantly higher mean number of visits to their primary care clinic and diagnostic services than men. Mean charges for primary care, specialty care, emergency treatment, diagnostic services, and annual total charges were all significantly higher for women than men; however, there were no differences for mean hospitalizations or hospital charges.

Because the ACA requires insurance companies to charge the same rates regardless of gender, men will no longer get the discounts. This will result in higher premiums as the costs shift.

THE IMPACT OF MANDATES

The situation for men and women without insurance is the same. However, once again, demographics intrude and skew things toward men taking up more of the overall costs. Since insurance is mandated for everyone, it all seems fair on the surface. However, disparities in who pays for what matter a great deal. Here are four categories of insured people to consider:

1. Those who receive insurance through employment

2. Those who receive insurance based on age, disability, military status, or other circumstance

3. Those who need to purchase a policy but qualify for a discount because of income (Medicaid or something similar)

4. Those who must purchase a policy but do not qualify under Medicaid or other program for a subsidy

Of those categories, number four will necessarily see the greatest change and pay the highest costs. Estimates are that this group consists of nine million Americans—those who are not impoverished and who are relatively healthy. Their current health status means most do not carry any insurance at all—they see no need to do so, and paying premiums out-of-pocket seems like a waste of money. But under Obamacare, they will have to purchase insurance or pay a penalty.

The importance of this situation for men becomes apparent when it is understood that the fourth group outlined in the preceding list consists of more males than females. Their participation in Obamacare is needed so that risk (and cost) is spread across a larger pool. In other words, those that don't use the services help pay for those that do.

How skewed is this demographic? Exact figures are unknown, largely because this group is invisible to the health care system. They aren't getting checkups or receiving services on a regular basis. Many might show up at an ER only when they are bleeding or something is broken. They tend to pay as they go, and try to limit how much medical care they buy. This demographic is not being checked or screened for common medical conditions.

The current estimate is that those falling into this group break down to 45 percent women and 55 percent men. While not a striking difference at first, there are two other considerations. The first we have already seen: women tend to use health care (when available) at a much higher rate than men. The second has to do with how welfare benefits are doled out: those with children are more likely to qualify for and receive benefits, and single women with children are much more common than single men with children.

WHAT'S COVERED FOR MEN?

Obamacare mandates a suite of preventive care services for both men and women; however, the list is much longer for women. These services come without co-pay or deductible. A few are directed primarily at men:

- A one-time ultrasound aneurysm screening for men over sixty-five who have ever smoked
- Aspirin therapy for cardiovascular disease prevention in men aged forty-five to seventy-nine, when there is no significant danger of stomach bleeding
- Cholesterol screening for men over thirty-five and for any man with an increased risk for coronary artery disease

Other mandated benefits, such as high blood pressure screening, obesity counseling, and checks for colorectal cancer are not gender specific, but many of the newly covered preventive care measures will be offered only to women and children.

As a group, men fare less well under Obamacare than women or children, but the true effect depends less on gender alone and more on other factors and categories. Factors such as preexisting conditions and attitudes toward health care may bump up usage for a particular adult male, while his employment status and eligibility for subsidized insurance will affect how much a man is actually paying in premiums.

The differences between men and women under Obamacare largely evaporate as age increases, since many of the medical services for women are directed at women of childbearing age and those who become pregnant.

CHAPTER 10

Young Adults, Ages Eighteen to Twenty-Nine

This age group is an essential demographic under Obamacare. It will feel the brunt of the changes financially, while not necessarily gaining many advantages. In some respects, the ACA treats young adults the same way Social Security does: they are a resource on the payment side without being a burden on the benefits side of the ledger.

Social Security is an income insurance program that relies on payments from younger Americans to keep it solvent. Younger workers pay in, but not many of them collect benefits while still young. In the same way, the ACA is partially funded by young adults who pay for health insurance they rarely use. By mandating coverage, the premiums paid increase the pool without increasing overall costs. The net result is that those who use health insurance (the elderly, the very young, and the infirm) will pay lower premiums than they otherwise would have to.

HOW WILL YOU OBTAIN INSURANCE?

While being forced to buy insurance when you are healthy and do not anticipate using it seems unfair, there are several paths to getting insurance that make it less expensive. One is that adults aged twenty-six and under will be allowed to continue on a parent's insurance plan. This feature is set in the

ACA, and coverage obtained this way is usually better and cheaper than getting insurance on your own. Whether or not you pay for it yourself depends on whether your parents intend to pay your premiums or whether they want you to contribute.

The ability to remain on a parent's plan is not affected by your status as a student, your income, your employment status (even if your employer offers insurance), or even if you are married. Previously, young adults had to be dependents for tax purposes for them to remain insured on a parent's policy. Now, anyone is eligible up to age twenty-six.

Without the restriction of being a dependent or living with parents, some odd combinations emerge. For example, a young man, aged twenty-four, could be on his mother's policy, even if he is married, has a good job, and his wife also works. In fact, his spouse could be on *her* parent's insurance as well. After twenty-six years old, each would have to obtain health insurance through other means, and this would depend on employment and total family income.

YOUNG ADULTS ON THEIR OWN

If you are not covered under a parent's policy, or you are older than twenty-six, you will have to purchase health insurance on your own. If you are low income, you may qualify for a subsidy or even full coverage. Those who make less than 133 percent of the federal poverty line (FPL) and who live in a participating state will be eligible for health insurance through Medicaid. Over that amount, but under 400 percent of the FPL, subsidies are available to buy a policy through an insurance exchange. Another option is getting insurance through an employer, if available.

Young adults who are living independently (without a parent's plan to rely on) are most likely to feel the pinch. This demographic will generally not be at their highest earning level yet, may still be burdened by student loan debt, and are more likely to be working part-time jobs where no insurance coverage is offered. For a single individual, the 2013 FPL is $11,490 a year. This would trigger full health care benefits, with Medicaid eligibility up to $15,282, the 133 percent FPL mark, provided one's state of residence has accepted the federal government's offer.

From 133 percent through 400 percent of FPL ($45,960 in the above example), some subsidies will be given. These come on a sliding scale and are intended to allow you to purchase a policy on the state insurance exchange. Exchanges are set up to provide health care policies from the lowest cost/lowest benefits, through to higher cost policies with more coverage.

CATASTROPHIC HEALTH INSURANCE

There is one other option. If you only want to meet the requirements of the individual mandate, a plan that provides minimal coverage will be available. This so-called "catastrophic insurance" is meant to have the lowest possible premiums while still covering extreme circumstances. However, because it has to qualify under Obamacare, even catastrophic insurance policies will cover three annual visits to your primary-care doctor and some preventive health services.

On average, a catastrophic policy will cover less than 60 percent of estimated health care costs. But this number is calculated from the health care costs of the entire population. Young adults use health care much less, and in this demographic, a catastrophic plan may meet their entire need.

Catastrophic policies will be offered only to single individuals (not families) who are under thirty years of age.

WILL YOUNG PEOPLE BENEFIT AT ALL FROM HAVING TO BUY HEALTH INSURANCE?

Under the ACA, there are a few new benefits of interest to young adults. Although much more is covered (and must be covered under any plan offered), only a couple of benefits are expected to be heavily used in this segment of the population.

Birth control and pregnancy care are utilized more in this age group than any other. Prenatal benefits, well-woman appointments and care, and maternity benefits are all included at some level in all policies. Wellness and preventive care (things like Pap smears and physicals) are covered at no charge. Birth control pills are covered, and no co-pays can be charged for prescriptions.

Sexual health is a covered benefit. A wide range of sexually transmitted diseases will be tested for without charge. Counseling on sexual health is also a covered benefit.

Addiction is a problem more prevalent in young adults, and benefits under Obamacare address this. Starting in 2014, substance use disorders will be covered. Exactly what type of treatment, and how much will be covered, remains to be determined as of July 2013. The Department of Health and Human Services (HHS) is due to publish guidelines by January of 2014.

One final, but significant, benefit comes when a young person is diagnosed with a serious, chronic ailment. While these conditions are not as common in this age group, they certainly do happen. Insurance policies under the ACA limit how much you can be charged in a single year (starting in 2014) and remove caps on coverage, so that a policy doesn't "limit out" and stop paying. For those who are unfortunate enough to be stricken, having a policy in place may prevent bankruptcy or an unsustainable financial drain.

CHAPTER 11

Parents with Children over Eighteen

The primary change under Obamacare for parents with adult children is that these children will now be eligible for coverage.

Previously, once children reached the age of eighteen, they could be dropped, unless they remained a dependent (for tax purposes) or were students in college. Even as students, adult children would be dropped from a policy at age twenty-four. The new guidelines allow you to keep adult children on your plan until the age of twenty-six—regardless of their status as a dependent.

In fact, other than their age, there are really no limiting factors. Adult children can remain on your policy even if they have moved out, are married, or if they have health insurance offered through an employer. Note that all individuals still require insurance; it's just a matter of where they get it.

SHOULD I KEEP MY CHILDREN ON MY POLICY?

The answer depends on whether or not your child will get a better deal if they stay on your policy or if they seek insurance on their own. If they are over twenty-six, the choice disappears, but between eighteen and twenty-six, you have options.

If your adult child still lives at home and you still support them financially, there are only two cases to consider. The first is whether or not they can get insurance through an employer. The second is the price of a policy through an insurance exchange.

If your adult child is working full-time and there is an employer-sponsored health insurance program in place, it becomes a matter of comparing your policy and the one offered. Since many employers contribute to an insurance plan, it may be less expensive for your children to get insurance through their work, even if you agree to pay the premiums for them.

If your child doesn't work, or has no access to an employer-sponsored plan, they are still eligible to get health insurance through an insurance exchange. Again, the decision is between premium costs and benefits. Since most young adults do not use health care as much as older (or very young) people, buying a policy with minimal coverage and the lowest possible premiums might make sense.

If your child is financially independent, they can still remain on your policy, but they might be eligible for a subsidy. Subsidies to help pay for insurance are available for those whose income is up to 400 percent of the federal poverty line (FPL). Using 2013 figures, this means an individual living on their own (not a dependent on someone else's taxes) can get money if they make less than $45,960. Higher subsidies are paid as income falls, with full coverage kicking in (for an individual) with an annual income of about $15,000.

Adult children who qualify for subsidies (or for Medicaid directly) are likely to get a better deal on their own than if they remained on your health insurance. And it may be cheaper for you to pay their subsidized premium than to continue to pay for them through your plan.

CATASTROPHIC HEALTH INSURANCE

Since young adults use less health insurance as a group, Obamacare includes a provision to offer them a catastrophic insurance plan—one meant to cover those rare instances where a devastating illness or injury occurs.

These plans are offered through insurance exchanges and are available only to those under the age of thirty. Their purpose is to meet the minimal requirements of a qualifying plan at the lowest possible cost.

When considering a switch to a catastrophic health care policy, it's important to look at the benefits and evaluate the plan based on services, not just premiums. All insurance policies, including a catastrophic policy, will cover some essential health benefits (EHBs), including preventive services. But plans will vary when it comes to things like deductibles, hospitalization, and all the various services you may be covered for under your current plan. Make sure to look at vision, dental, and other items your child may need when making the decision.

OTHER CONSIDERATIONS

If you are taking a substantial tax deduction because you pay for an adult child's health insurance, this may no longer be available to you. The IRS is still drawing up rules for penalties and credits under Obamacare, and you will see the changes in the 2014 tax year, unless things get put on hold.

If your child has a preexisting condition that made them ineligible for insurance, or kept them from switching to a new carrier, there's good news. Preexisting conditions are no longer a way for insurance companies to drop coverage.

Adult children who are seasonal or contract workers will fare the worst under Obamacare, especially if they make a decent income. The rules do not capture a "flexible" worker because they assume steady employment. In this case, your adult child will either have to remain on your plan (if they are under twenty-six) or buy health insurance directly.

CHAPTER 12

Children Under Eighteen

Because Obamacare focuses on prevention, checkups and screenings are key features. Several services are directed at catching childhood diseases or medical problems early. These standards are generated by the U.S. Preventive Services Task Force (USPSTF), the Centers for Disease Control (CDC), and the Department of Health and Human Services (HHS).

PREVENTIVE SERVICES

There are several changes in the insurance marketplace that directly impact minors. The first is that insurers cannot charge a co-pay or deductible on preventive services. These medical treatments include the following:

- Immunizations—based on CDC recommendations. There are currently fourteen vaccinations that children receive before eighteen years of age. Some of these are given multiple times as a sequence over several years, and others only once. See the CDC website (http://www.cdc.gov/mmwr/preview/mmwrhtml/su6201a2.htm) for the complete list of recommendations.
- Pediatrician visits for checkups and screenings
- Counseling for childhood obesity (parents and children)
- Annual flu shots
- Vision and hearing screening (testing and referrals)

- Dental care prevention for preschool children, including recommending fluoride supplements for those older than six months, where water supplies are deficient
- Depression screening for adolescents (twelve to eighteen years old) where expertise for diagnosis and treatment are available
- Sickle cell screening for all newborns
- Hypothyroid screening for newborns
- Iron supplementation at six to twelve months for babies at risk of deficiency
- Phenylketonuria screening for newborns
- Skin cancer counseling—meant to educate children about sun expose to minimize risk (ages ten to twenty-four) and primarily focused on those with pale skin
- Vision screening to test for amblyopia (lazy eye) once between three and five years of age

All of these services are set as minimal standards for all qualifying insurance coverage. They are based on "best practices" set by the CDC, the USPSTF, and other federal health care entities.

STATES VERSUS FEDERAL GOVERNMENT

The preceding list states the current minimums that policies must provide at no additional charge; however, state-level programs often differ, leading to a collision between federal and state standards for child insurance coverage.

One change with Obamacare had a particular impact: the requirement that children be offered coverage under a parent or guardian's policy. Because of this, states anticipated a shift away from benefit programs under welfare and into the private market. The ACA addresses this specifically, mandating that states continue to cover existing recipients.

A combination program (with both state and federal funding), the Children's Health Insurance Program (CHIP), was even part of a U.S. Supreme Court case, with the Court coming down on the side of Obamacare rules. The result is that low-income families with qualifying children cannot be disenrolled by states, even if the state has a budget shortfall. States must continue to provide services under the program until at least 2019. CHIP is a popular program that covers children for ER visits, hospitalization, prescription drugs, and other services.

Other than CHIP, benefits at the state level for children will be set by essential health benefits (EHBs) through insurance exchanges in a manner similar to other policies.

EHBs and Children

An EHB list has been published by the HHS. The ruling, which came out in the spring of 2013, outlines the minimum services that all private policies must offer as EHBs. If a policy doesn't meet one or more of the minimums, they must be offered as a separate policy in a state's insurance exchange.

For example, if there isn't a private carrier in a state's insurance exchange offering vision screening at no charge, a separate offering must be created to do so. The purpose of this provision is to allow all children to have access to these services.

How Much Will It Cost Parents?

Although some services are mandated without co-pays or deductibles and must be included in qualified plans, premiums are not set. Rather, private insurance carriers are allowed to set rates on a state-by-state basis. This also governs the details of what services, beyond the basics, will be covered. A policy may, for instance, have a benefit covering glasses for children in one state but not in another.

OTHER STIPULATIONS

One huge change that is already in effect under Obamacare is that insurers are not allowed to deny or drop coverage for preexisting conditions. Until 2014, they may charge more for such coverage, but afterward, a child on a policy with a preexisting condition will not generate a premium increase. There is also an exception for policies that do not cover children. (This also goes away in 2014 when all policies must allow for children.)

Preexisting conditions in children have been a terrible burden on families, and the ACA addresses this with a national "high-risk pool program." Under section 101 of the ACA, this pool is meant to provide a buffer until parents can obtain other insurance for their child. The reason is that there may be a substantial waiting period (as much as a year) until a private carrier will cover a preexisting condition. The pool is meant to fill in this gap, and the program itself phases out by 2017, with the expectation that all children will have become insured by then.

Two current situations will also be phased out in 2014. The first, also focused on preexisting conditions, offered a high-premium policy to those who have been denied private insurance because of a preexisting condition, both adults and children. The second is a mechanism whereby insurance carriers could deny coverage for specific procedures under an "exclusion." An exclusion would restrict coverage, for example, on repeating a procedure that had already been performed once, such as a disc surgery. The idea was to avoid paying multiple times for similar medical procedures. Both of these disappear in 2014, with the expectation that insurance exchanges will make these moot.

The key changes for children's coverage under Obamacare are:

- More basic services covered (no co-pay or fee), with the idea of preventing or detecting developmental conditions
- Essential health benefits set national standards of care
- State standards on other services and the costs will vary
- Children will have to be covered under a parent or guardian's policy
- Benefits under CHIP cannot be dropped
- Preexisting conditions cannot be used to deny coverage

The expectation is that premiums for private health insurance will rise because of these requirements, but how much they will go up is unknown.

CHAPTER 13

Seniors and Current Medicare Users

If you were looking for a government program to rival the ACA in complexity, Medicare would be it. From its creation under the Social Security Act in the 1960s until now, Medicare has only grown. In fact, it's a huge elephant in the room when it comes to health care in the United States. Any attempt to change the way we pay for health care in America has to address the political hot potato of Medicare head on.

BEFORE OBAMACARE

Medicare is a health insurance plan offered to any U.S. citizen when they reach sixty-five years old, which they can use for twenty years. As first enacted, Medicare was designed to address the problem of hospitalization costs for seniors. At the time, hospitalization was the largest chunk of what an older person could expect to pay for health care. In some cases, a single stint in the hospital could cripple them financially, and many were going bankrupt because of hospital bills.

But the health care system changed over time. Hospitalization, although still significant, is no longer the primary concern. Instead, other costs have emerged to drain the financial resources of retirees. Out-of-pocket payments for medical devices, nonhospital medical care, and prescription drugs led to additions to Medicare. The program now includes parts A, B, C, and D, each of which targets a different area of health care costs. The latest, part D, was enacted in 2007 as a prescription drug benefit. At the time, the financial drain of paying for prescriptions was forcing some seniors to decide between purchasing needed medicine or buying food.

Supplemental policies are also offered to seniors to fill various gaps in coverage. Like Medicare itself, supplemental policies require some payments for seniors, making Medicare and its variations much different than Medicaid, where almost all costs are borne by public funding.

One further addition, Medicare Advantage, offered a blend of privately and publicly funded health insurance. Seniors could customize the coverage they wanted by purchasing a policy, and the government would supplement the cost. Additional services such as vision or hearing could be added on, although this meant paying a higher premium.

THE DONUT HOLE

For prescription drug coverage, Medicare part D has a cost-sharing element that kicks in when a deductible is reached. The deductible is set at a few hundred dollars. After this is met, and up to a cap of $2,800, a senior would pay only 25 percent of a drug's cost. The "donut hole" referred to what happened after this cap was reached. From $2,800 to $6,400, Medicare pays nothing toward drug costs. Above the second amount, the drug benefit kicks in again, now paying 95 percent of the cost. The middle area, where no coverage exists, is called the donut hole. The ACA fills this.

Filling the hole is accomplished by a combination of contributions from the federal government (25 percent) and drug companies (50 percent) so the net paid by seniors remains at 25 percent. The hole goes away.

Not all of this kicks in at once. Instead, the hole is gradually closed over time, dropping from 100 percent (donut hole) to 50 percent in 2013 and then fully closing by 2020.

MEDICARE REFORMS

Obamacare is partially funded by reforms to Medicare. Primarily, these reforms come through reduced payments for services, including lowering the amounts by which Medicare Advantage is subsidized. For the one in four seniors who have Medicare Advantage, this is not good news. Their premiums will rise, or the benefits offered will fall.

The thinking, in terms of the legislation, is to recover inefficiencies in the system and lower payments to doctors and hospitals. No one knows what effect this will have. When reimbursement falls, there is less incentive to accept a patient with Medicare. On the other hand, Medicare is so huge that it will be hard to completely ignore this segment of the market.

Other cuts come in services Medicare will pay for. In total, this is expected to generate more than a half-trillion dollars in savings over the next decade.

NEW TAXES

The money recovered through Medicare cuts will be used to fund increased services under Medicaid, but there are additional taxes that are also meant to add funding. The first is an increase on the Medicare taxes collected on wages, from 1.45 percent to 2.35 percent on individuals making more than $200,000.

Another tax increase is on capital gains above $250,000—an additional 3.8 percent. These two taxes shift some of the financial burden onto the more affluent Americans, but if you are well off, they will hit you, too.

A tax is also imposed on the manufacture and sale of medical devices. This is expected to be passed onto consumers. The 2.3 percent excise tax will also go into the Obamacare funding pool.

THE IPAB

The Independent Payment Advisory Board (IPAB) will influence how Medicare is shaped after 2015. This is when the board gains the authority to examine Medicare payments and set spending limits. Spending limits indirectly affect the care that seniors will receive, since doctors and hospitals are unlikely to offer services for free. The IPAB, when proposed, generated strong language and the term "death panel" because of this power. However, the statutory language that gives the IPAB its authority forbids it to recommend restricting care even as a broad policy measure—let alone in individual cases. Although the IPAB starts up in 2015, its first recommendations will not take effect until 2018.

OTHER CHANGES

Obamacare shifts the focus of health insurance toward preventive care. The idea is to catch diseases early, when they are cheaper to treat. For this reason, services such as blood pressure, bone density, and cholesterol checks will come with no co-pay or cost. Other services (like vaccinations, counseling for mental health issues, and annual checkups) also come with no out-of-pocket fees.

Another set of services, called essential health benefits, will also be covered. These changes have been incorporated into Medicare starting in 2011. More may be added based on scientific assessments of proven cost reductions. For example, if a cancer screening demonstrates an overall cost savings through early detection, it will be added as a no-cost benefit. Services mediated or regulated by states must meet the federally defined benefits, although specifics of delivery and cost may vary according to state rules already in place or still being developed.

CHAPTER 14

Insured Americans

If you already have health insurance, Obamacare may or may not alter your coverage or premiums. This section addresses those with traditional, private health care plans. If you are on Medicare or Medicaid, or if you are uninsured, you should read those sections instead.

In general, premiums will rise for private health insurance. The reasons are several, but one primary reason is that, under Obamacare, insurance companies are required to offer some services without a co-pay.

NO CO-PAY SERVICES

Obamacare puts an emphasis on preventive care. Things like breast cancer screenings, cholesterol tests, and wellness counseling have mandated coverage with no co-pay attached. The purpose of this is to allow cost savings down the road, because you are catching treatable conditions early enough to stave off higher-priced care later on.

There is some scientific validation for doing this, but it depends on people accessing health care when they don't necessarily feel sick. To encourage this, Obamacare introduces a set of free services. They are free to the patient at the point of delivery, but they still cost money. These costs are rolled into the premiums for private health insurance plans.

Not all private health care insurance will change. If your plan is grandfathered in, you will be able to keep it in place with the same level of coverage you have now. However, if you change to a new policy, it will include the provisions of Obamacare, and you will not be allowed to switch back. Grandfathered plans were in place in 2010 (or before) and do not have the premium increase protections mentioned below or the no co-pay services (unless they already had them).

No co-pay services under Obamacare will include the following:

- A yearly health checkup for women, including twenty-two different services. Most are screening-based (to check for a medical condition) or counseling on various aspects of health care for females.
- All adults have fifteen additional screenings offered, including high blood pressure checks, cholesterol and diabetes screening, and addiction counseling.
- There are twenty-two prevention services covered for children and adolescents, including vaccinations, hearing and vision checks, and some mental health services.

PREMIUM INCREASES UNDER OBAMACARE

Restrictions on premium increases went into effect in 2011 and have further changes coming in January 2014. Currently, insurance carriers are not allowed to raise their rates solely to make more profit. They have to justify increases based on increased costs. Hikes in premiums above 10 percent have to have a state-level review. They also have to meet an 80/20 rule: eighty percent of insurance premiums must be spent on health care. If they do not, they have to give customers a rebate to meet the rule.

If your insurance is through your employer, you could lose coverage altogether. Some employers might find it less costly to pay the fine for not providing insurance, rather than pay increased premiums. However, data from "Romneycare" in Massachusetts suggests that even when fines are lower than the cost of insurance, they combine with employer competitiveness to actually increase the number of employer-offered plans.

Current employment-based plans are customized by insurance carriers to meet market demands. To keep premiums low, they may have a high deductible, high co-pays, or limit coverage. Because Obamacare regulates what must be covered (including no co-pay services), an employment-based insurance plan may no longer be viable, or have premiums raised to match regulated coverage.

Some plans will have to pay a penalty beginning in 2018. The so-called "Cadillac" insurance plans, defined as those having a plan value higher than $10,200 for an individual or $27,500 for a family, will be taxed at a 40 percent rate for any value above those figures. The "plan value" is the total annual premium cost. Although the tax is levied against the insurance carrier, not the policyholder, such plans are likely to be phased out unless the extra charges can be passed along.

OTHER CHANGES

Under Obamacare, health savings accounts (HSAs) will have a 20 percent penalty when used for purchases that are not allowed, and the type of purchases allowed also changes. For example, over-the-counter medicines are no longer an allowable expense. If you use your HSA for such purchases, you will be levied a 20 percent tax for doing so. One work-around, where medications have both an over-the-counter and prescription variety is to get a prescription so that the medicine will be covered. Commonly, ulcer medications and allergy drugs come in both prescription and over-the-counter forms. One other tactic would be to get a letter of "medical necessity" from your doctor.

You will be required to document purchases made under an HSA or a flexible spending account (FSA) with a detailed receipt, and either a prescription (can be used for over-the-counter items as well) or a letter of medical necessity. If you purchase over-the-counter medications regularly, this is worth the trouble, but the expectation is that most consumers won't bother.

The amount of money an employer can contribute to an FSA gets a cap of $2,500 under Obamacare. These accounts are funded with pre-tax dollars, usually with employer-matched funds, and are used to pay for medical expenses (such as co-pays or deductibles) that were not covered. They have a "use it or lose it" provision. At the time of this publication, that provision was being debated.

FSAs and HSAs are commonly used to pay for deductibles. Under Obamacare, the maximum yearly deductible is also capped, making these plans less useful once the deductible is met. Caps are currently at $2,000 for singles and $4,000 for families.

A list of FSA-eligible expenses can be found at the Wage Works website (http://www.wageworks.com/employee/health-care/expenses/fsa.htm#A).

EXEMPTIONS

Some businesses have received waivers from Obamacare. More than one thousand waivers have been issued, with about half going to plans that service union members. The waivers have been controversial and all are set to expire in 2014.

If you are eligible for services through the Indian Health Service, you will not have to meet the individual mandate for Obamacare.

Certain religious groups are exempt because of their beliefs. Also exempt are groups that currently participate in a Health Care Sharing Ministry created before January 1, 2000. Both exemptions are narrowly defined by the law, and must have a historical basis that precedes the passage of the ACA by anywhere from one to three decades. One cannot simply cover a personal objection to the law under the rubric of religion.

CHAPTER 15

Americans with Employer-Sponsored Insurance

The largest category of insured Americans who currently have private health insurance get coverage through an employer. According to the Census Bureau, about 157 million U.S. citizens had employer-sponsored insurance (ESI) in 2009. While Obamacare's primary objective is to provide insurance for those without any, doing so has an impact on ESI. These unintended consequences have the potential to change ESI a great deal, but no one yet knows what will happen.

The timeline is also subject to change, with President Obama delaying some of the employer mandates that were due to take effect in 2014 until 2015 (this was changed in July 2013).

THE INDIVIDUAL MANDATE

A critical feature of the ACA is the requirement that everyone have health insurance. This means employers may no longer be the only or the best option available. Some employers may decide to stop offering health insurance with the expectation that their employees will access the new insurance exchanges and private market instead. The mandate, after all, is directed at individuals, not businesses.

Those that continue to offer coverage through employment might even be tempted to push employees out of a company plan—especially those who are eligible for subsidies. But the ACA has provisions in place meant to stop this migration and to keep ESI in place. The net result, if everything works as it should, is that those with ESI currently will see some changes in coverage (such as mandated benefits) and some changes in premiums (to cover mandated benefits), but otherwise, things will carry on as before.

MORE BENEFITS MEAN HIGHER PREMIUMS

Depending on the health coverage your employer provides, you are likely to see a rise in premiums as Obamacare takes effect. This is because certain minimal benefits are required, and policies that currently do not pay for these benefits must be "upgraded." But one person's upgrade is another's unnecessary benefit. So, for example, a policy that covers mental health services by mandate will cost more, even for those who aren't interested in having such coverage.

In some ways, the initial increase in premiums is a reflection of how prevalent discounted policies have become. An insurer who offers a plan with minimal benefits can charge much less for the policy, making it attractive to businesses and their employees who don't want to pay higher premiums. Other ways to keep premiums low are to make deductibles and co-pays higher.

Under Obamacare, minimum benefits are set. Any policy that relied on benefits below these minimums to keep premiums low will have to raise rates. This economic reality comes with a jump in premiums at first, but, as policies come into compliance, premiums are supposed to stabilize again. No one knows for certain if this will happen. Early data from states that set up their marketplaces early, or engaged in active negotiations as buyers of insurance, indicate that such stabilization may be taking place.

GRANDFATHERED PLANS

Employers with a plan in place in 2010 are able to continue offering it, at least through 2014. These plans might not meet the standards of the ACA, but are "grandfathered" in. If you are enrolled in a grandfathered plan, your coverage and premiums should change only minimally until 2014.

The old plans are still regulated by Obamacare, and employers can only make small changes without losing the grandfathered status. In particular, there are restrictions on how much premiums can rise and there are limits on cost sharing. The end result is that grandfathered plans will gradually become less and less attractive to employees. Over time, these plans lose the ability to compete with plans that are allowed to change with circumstances.

MORE COSTS

Realizing that costs rise with new services is fundamental to understanding how Obamacare will affect those covered by ESIs. Adding benefits means rates rise, and these will have to be picked up by an employer or the employee who pays for their health care.

Two of the predicted drivers of increased costs are administrative and reporting requirements. These started appearing on W-2 forms in 2011 but weren't mandatory until 2012. Other reports are sent to the IRS (or other agencies) directly, and by 2014, employers will be providing all the needed reports necessary to enforce the individual mandate.

Preventive health services mandated by the ACA will be included in non-grandfathered policies and represent another way increased benefits will increase premiums. These services must be included in qualifying plans, and include screenings for diabetes and high blood pressure, as well as other basic checkups, vaccinations, and a long list of services for women of childbearing age and for children.

In some states, these preventive services will be subsidized, but the general expectation is increased premiums for ESIs. Changes in income levels that qualify for Medicaid will mean some employees will do better financially by not paying for ESI or by having a spouse (or child) get benefits while they do not.

PAY OR PLAY

For some employers, it will cost less to pay a penalty for not providing ESI than to provide it. Employers may decide to pay the fine instead of "playing the game." Fines are levied as a tax on a per-employee basis, and these will rise over time. But if your employer decides to pay instead of play, you may lose your insurance benefits altogether.

If your employer drops coverage and pays the penalty, you are still responsible for maintaining health insurance. The individual mandate attaches to individuals, not employers.

However dire this seems at first glance, many employers already contribute less to health plans than the penalties, so there is no incentive for them to drop coverage. They may also try paying more for workers with low wages and let higher-wage workers contribute more. Doing this would allow them to shift costs around and retain coverage for everyone.

The best bet for those with employer-sponsored health insurance is to be aware of what new benefits are allowed and keep an eye on premiums being charged. As part of Obamacare, employers and insurance companies are required to keep you informed of changes and costs. Read the information you are given and ask questions to avoid frustration and surprises.

CHAPTER 16

Large Business Employees

One of the stated purposes of the ACA is to insure Americans who don't have access to affordable health care. The model for coverage was actually derived from standard offerings that large corporations have in place now. Because of their size, these businesses have the economic muscle to negotiate the best deals for their employees, and these policies became the basis for what Obamacare attempts to make available to everyone.

A large business is defined as a company with more than fifty full-time workers. Part-time employees still count though: for every 120 hours a month in part-time wages paid, the full-time count goes up by one. This prevents companies from hiring only part-time labor to avoid Obamacare.

CHANGES TO EXISTING POLICIES

Those that receive health insurance through a large company (the normal situation among employed Americans) will see few changes. Estimates are that only 3 percent of large businesses will have to make substantial modifications. However, there are still some details worth noting.

Obamacare doesn't alter your current employer-sponsored insurance (ESI) directly. It is illegal for the federal government to do so—as settled in a Supreme Court challenge to Obamacare. This is because health insurance is regulated at the state level. Each state can decide how insurance is to be sold within their borders.

So how does Obamacare modify the insurance landscape? By taxing employers who do not meet the guidelines for health insurance, the ACA influences the choices employers are likely to make. They are able to do this because federal tax law provisions already address the money a corporation spends to offer health insurance to their employees. By modifying the tax burden, Obamacare also pushes employers to modify the policies they offer.

In the end, the changes you are most likely to see are increased benefits for preventive services (with no co-pay or fees) and some additional services. You are also likely to see an increase in premiums because the benefits have to be paid for.

EMPLOYER MANDATES

The mandate under Obamacare is an individual one. This means that the bottom line is on the individual to get, pay for, and keep a qualifying health insurance policy. However, if employers wish to offer a policy to their workers (and avoid paying penalties), they must meet certain guidelines. These guidelines are referred to as the employer mandate.

Remember, employers are *not required* to meet the guidelines. In fact, they aren't even required to offer health insurance at all. What's actually happening is that employers choose to offer health benefits because they get a huge tax break for doing so. Money spent on employer-sponsored health care is not subject to the taxes that regular wages are.

The same logic applies when your employer wants to avoid the tax penalties for not following all the policy guidelines under Obamacare. Instead, they will seek to make their policies match the standard ACA offerings. This keeps them in compliance and saves the company money. In the end, the goals aren't mandated, but they'll be met anyhow.

COVERAGE CHANGES

Some of the coverage changes have already taken place. Birth control no longer comes with a co-pay. Family members are offered coverage and children can remain on a policy until the age of twenty-six. These and other changes provide a flood of essential health benefits (EHBs) that policies must cover to avoid penalties.

Other changes come if you have a health savings account (HSA) (also knowns as a flexible spending account, or FSA) through your employer. These accounts provide a tax-free way to pay for deductibles and co-pays. The ACA sets limits on how large these accounts can be.

As we have mentioned, premiums are likely to rise under Obamacare, at least initially. But ESI premiums can't simply increase without limit. Your costs cannot exceed 9.5 percent of your income. If premiums exceed that amount, the plan will not qualify.

Finally, there are limits set on deductibles and cost sharing. These are sometimes used to artificially lower premiums (insurers recoup this lower revenue on the back end, as services are used).

IF YOU ARE EMPLOYED WITH NO EMPLOYER-SPONSORED HEALTH INSURANCE

In some situations, a large company has a high percentage of workers who are not on a company health plan and who don't make enough to afford private insurance. This situation arises in the fast-food industry, with big-box retailers, and in industries with traditionally low wages. You may work for a company like this, or you may be a part-time worker and not enrolled in a company plan. If so, you would be able to buy health insurance through an insurance exchange. Each state will vary a bit on what specific policies are offered, but if you are unable to pay for a policy, you will probably qualify for a subsidy.

Subsidies are based on income and are given to reduce the overall policy cost to the consumer. Subsidies are calculated against the federal poverty line (FPL), with those making up to 400 percent of this number eligible for something.

For example, the FPL for a family of four is $23,550 (in 2013). Subsidies would then be available for this family up to a total income of $94,200. Currently a full subsidy is given at 133 percent of the FPL, meaning the same family (if they made only $31,322) would be able to get health insurance for free through either an exchange premium reimbursement or directly through Medicaid.

Large companies are currently not allowed to access the insurance exchanges, although by 2017 they will have access in at least some states. When this happens, your policy may switch to a lower-cost version through an exchange, although the mechanism of payment (withdrawal from your paycheck) will not.

UNION WORKERS

Health insurance is generally part of a negotiated union contract. Until 2012, union-negotiated health insurance was not subject to the provisions of Obamacare. However, the exemption has since expired. Unions may have "hybrid" plans. These are paid by employers when a union member is working, but coverage continues in off-seasons or when the union member is unemployed. The union acts as the administrator.

How these hybrid plans will be affected is still to be determined. The expectation is that union members who are essentially part-time workers will use the insurance exchanges and subsidies instead of the current, union-administered plans. However, all this is subject to contract negotiations, making it complex.

CHAPTER 17

Small Business Employees

If you are employed by a business with fifty or fewer full-time employees, you are considered to be working for a small business. This is unrelated to how much you are paid or how much a business earns.

MANDATES

While your employer is not required to offer you health insurance, you are still required to have it. If your employer does offer a plan, it will have to meet certain basic requirements. If they do not have insurance as a benefit, you will have to purchase insurance on your own that meets the minimum standards.

It is a myth that under Obamacare all employers have to offer health insurance to their employees.

FULL- OR PART-TIME EMPLOYEES

Many small businesses get by with a higher percentage of part-time workers than larger businesses do. If you work part-time, your employer does not have to offer you employer-sponsored insurance, even if they do offer it to full-time employees. The dividing line between full- and part-time under the ACA is an average of thirty hours a week calculated on a monthly basis (120 hours a month). An employee may work more than thirty hours in any particular week and still be part-time, as long as they stay under the monthly minimum.

This leads to circumstances where an employed person is still out shopping to meet the individual mandate. Even with multiple jobs, so long as you are not full-time at any one of them, you will need to get insurance on your own. In cases where another family member is employed with insurance, you will be allowed to participate in their coverage.

HOW WILL IT WORK IN MY CIRCUMSTANCES?

Small businesses are treated differently than large businesses under the ACA, but the differences are mostly invisible to workers. Instead of thinking of your situation as small business vs. large, it's better to examine which other categories you and your family fall under.

All of these categories are covered in this book. You should read any that apply to you, because they will have a greater impact than your employment.

- **Insured by employer or not?** This will determine whether you have to purchase insurance yourself through an insurance exchange.
- **Family circumstances** will determine whether or not you will be covered under someone else's policy, and along with income, what subsidies you qualify for.
- **Income level** sets the mark for subsidies on premiums. Citizens who earn up to 400 percent of the federal poverty line (FPL) qualify for some payments. These subsidies are used to buy health insurance (when not offered by an employer), and the amount is determined on a sliding scale based on income.
- **Very low income** (less than 133 percent of the FPL) for a family will, in most states, allow you to receive benefits under Medicaid. If you have children, they may be covered under the Children's Health Insurance Program (CHIP).

- **Your age** may determine whether you can be a dependent under a parent's policy (twenty-six years old or younger), whether you qualify for a special, low-cost, catastrophic policy (under thirty years old), or whether you qualify for Medicare (over sixty-five years old).

Look over the contents of Part III of this book, and read any sections that apply to you to find out more details.

WHAT IF I HAVE INSURANCE?

If you have employer-sponsored insurance (ESI), or you are getting insurance through your spouse, the changes you will see depend on the coverage. Again, this has little to do with whether the insurance is through a small or a large employer. For most, premiums will initially rise, but then level off.

Increased premiums come from two major factors. The first is additional benefits under Obamacare that all qualifying policies have to meet. These new benefits add to the value of a policy, but they also increase the costs. The second factor is a lowering of allowed deductibles. Some insurance policies use higher deductibles (and cost sharing) to lower premium rates. In most cases, this will no longer be allowed. Other restrictions, such as mandating coverage for existing conditions and disallowing cancellation of a policy for mistakes (called *rescission,* and historically subject to abuse), also tend to increase premiums.

The plateau in premium increases is expected once policies are standardized and insurance companies begin to compete for business in insurance exchanges. Premium increases are also regulated under the ACA. Eventually, this should mean a more stable, affordable market for health insurance. Other costs, such as treatment costs, may continue to push premiums higher, but these shouldn't generate increases as dramatic as some fear for this stage of implementation.

If you get your insurance through a small business, you may actually see your premiums go *down*. This happens when a small business gains access to a special insurance exchange designed to pool their buying power with other small businesses. This exchange is called SHOP (Small Business Health Options Program).

It is estimated that health insurance currently costs small businesses as much as 18 percent more than the same coverage through a large business plan. If your employer can recover savings at this level, and they pass the savings on to you, your premiums may actually go down. After some threatened delays due to technical issues, the SHOP exchange has gone online. However, its full value to small business (compared to traditional purchases through agents and brokers) may not be fully implemented for another year. In some states full implementation starts earlier, and some insurers are already offering qualifying coverage to small businesses to anticipate the change. Small business owners, as always, need to carefully comparison shop across their range of options.

CHAPTER 18

Unemployed Americans

Those who are unemployed are not distinguished as a special class under the ACA. Instead, the individual mandate still applies, and you will still have to obtain health insurance. The options then sort out by income level and whether or not you are eligible for insurance under a family member's policy.

COBRA

The ACA doesn't directly alter how the Consolidated Omnibus Reconciliation Act (COBRA) works. The recently unemployed are still eligible to continue employer-sponsored insurance (ESI) policies, just as before. However, since the employer no longer contributes to the cost, this option means a huge increase in premiums. This has always been a problem with COBRA, and most newly unemployed people will do better with another option.

There are a few circumstances when accessing COBRA makes sense. The first is when you expect to pick up new employment fairly quickly. In this case, a COBRA policy will fill the short gap in coverage while you are unemployed. A second scenario comes up when a spouse is generating significant income but doesn't have employer-sponsored insurance. For example, a spouse who is a freelancer or subcontractor, or who is a seasonal worker. Some couples rely on one employer primarily for the benefits and another for the income.

COBRA allows you to keep the same coverage, doctors, and health care network. If this is of primary importance, keeping a current policy may be worth the extra cost. In most cases, a COBRA policy extension will represent a pricier option than other ways to get coverage.

INCOME-BASED OPTIONS

As employment status isn't considered under Obamacare, the more relevant factor is family income, and your options are driven primarily by how much you and any family members make.

If your family income falls in the low-income range, calculated based on the federal poverty line (FPL), you may be eligible for Medicaid. Eligibility will depend on whether your state has chosen to participate in Medicaid expansion. The actual cutoff is 133 percent of the FPL, an increase under Obamacare. Medicaid coverage has been expanded under the ACA, but changing from a private policy to Medicaid can bring a switch in doctors, network, and coverage—something you will have to carefully evaluate.

If your family income (including unemployment benefits) falls between 133 and 400 percent of the FPL, you will still receive some help in purchasing insurance. Policies on the state-level insurance exchange will be offered at four price points and levels of coverage. Any subsidy you get will have to go toward paying premiums on one of these four plans, ranked as Platinum, Gold, Silver, and Bronze. For single individuals under thirty, there will be another option—a "catastrophic" health insurance, offered at the lowest cost but also with minimal coverage. All of these policies, except the catastrophic plan, can be used for a family as well as an individual.

If your family income is above the 400 percent FPL cutoff, you will still be able use the insurance exchanges, but you won't get any subsidy to do so.

GETTING ON A FAMILY MEMBER'S INSURANCE

If another family member is employed and has health coverage through their job, you can be added to their policy. Employers who offer health insurance have to allow this. The premiums your family member pays will go up as a result, but this is generally a better option than getting insurance as an individual.

If you are twenty-six years old or younger, you can even be added to a parent's policy. This option is a change under Obamacare, and it doesn't matter if you are living with your parents or even if you are married. (Your spouse will not be eligible to get coverage under your parents.) While complicated, this method of meeting the individual mandate is built into the ACA to meet the needs of younger adults who often find themselves between jobs.

FULL-TIME TO PART-TIME EMPLOYMENT

Some employers will shift their hiring strategy to increase the number of part-time workers. This has some advantage to them because part-time workers do not have to be offered health insurance. Since employers pay a percentage of insurance premiums, this savings can amount to a significant impact on their bottom-line profits.

If you are downgraded and move from full-time to part time, you will share the same difficulties as someone who is unemployed. The burden is still on you, as an individual, to obtain health insurance. The choices available are the same as those listed in the preceding list, and are are largely dependent on your family's income: Medicaid, insurance exchange with subsidy, and insurance exchange without subsidy.

SPECIAL CIRCUMSTANCES

An insurance option not covered earlier is available under special conditions, depending on your career and membership in a professional organization. Private insurance, not affiliated with an insurance exchange or employment, has been available to those in certain professions or through unions.

If you are a union member, you may have access to health insurance through your union benefits, regardless of employment status. Other organizations, usually based on profession, may also offer insurance policies. When the ACA was first enacted, some of these policies were exempt from coverage minimums and could offer less-than-standard coverage at a lower cost. These exemptions have expired (or will by 2014), and policies offered going forward will have to at least match those in an insurance exchange. Still, this is an option to consider, and you should check prices and availability.

UNEMPLOYMENT UNDER OBAMACARE

Critics of Obamacare predict the employer mandate (the insurance they must offer to avoid a tax penalty) will force more workers into the part-time segment of the workforce. So far (as of 2013), this hasn't happened. Employers have always had the option of hiring full- or part-time workers, and they seem willing to pay the extra expense for the full-time workers.

Another prediction is that once unemployed, workers will have a more difficult time getting new employment, as traditional "filler" jobs will now either be strictly part-time or cost an employer more to take on a full-time worker. For some types of jobs this is true. Low-wage jobs in particular, where health insurance would add significant costs (on a percentage basis) come with a disincentive to hire full-time workers. The question is how much the job market is driven by this factor and how much is shaped by the economic health of the nation overall.

If this prediction turns out to be accurate and unemployment rises, the health care system will be stressed under Obamacare. More families will be getting subsidies or free care (under Medicaid). If unemployment rates fall, the insurance burden will shift back to employers and employees, and government payouts will drop.

CHAPTER 19

Wealthy Adults

The wealthy, under Obamacare, includes those who are at the upper reaches of middle class, as well as the truly affluent. In many respects, this demographic will be burdened with the increased coverages under the ACA, mostly by way of higher taxes, but also because of some penalties placed on "Cadillac" health insurance.

WHO COUNTS AS WEALTHY?

Income and employment status are the two major shapers of how the ACA plays out in practice for any particular individual or family. While there is no definition of "wealthy" that everyone agrees on, for the purposes of understanding Obamacare, we will use the "bright lines" built into the act to reduce ambiguity. These show up as taxes imposed on families making more than $250,000 or individuals making more than $200,000 a year.

New taxes and payments from this group are intended to offset expanded Medicaid benefits for poorer Americans and help subsidize health insurance for lower middle-class earners as well. The taxes levied reflect another definition of wealthy that is not stated but still in play. That's the idea that the wealthy have large interest and dividend incomes and that they use existing tax policy in creative ways to get more than a fair share of health care. Whether you agree with that picture or not, it does inform what legislation changed under Obamacare.

NEW TAXES AND TAX CHANGES

Funding that flows from the wealthy to fund an expansion of insurance for the less well-off comes from increased taxes on interest and dividend income, and an increase in the tax rate on Medicare. The latter isn't a new tax, but the rate is.

The top tax rates for capital gains and dividends will go up from 15 to 18.8 percent for the 2013 tax year. These numbers will reflect the current tax situation and will change as other sections of the tax law change. For example, if Bush-era tax reform is dropped, the numbers go up. Under fiscal cliff legislation, those earning $400,000 and more saw a jump in taxation for capital gains and dividend income (up to 20 percent). The best way to capture this increase is to just add 3.8 percent onto whatever the rate would have been without Obamacare.

A second tax is applied directly against earned income. For income over $200,000 for an individual and $250,000 for a family, the Medicare tax will increase by 0.9 percent. The combination of these two tax increases is expected to raise a total of $468 billion over the next seven years (the life of the ACA).

If you are involved in the manufacture or sales of medical devices, a new tax has been imposed amounting to 2.3 percent of the price of the item. The tax also applies to importers of such devices.

CHANGES TO FLEXIBLE SPENDING ACCOUNTS

One criticism of the health insurance landscape that existed before Obama-care centered on how the wealthy used flexible spending accounts (FSA) compared to how lower-income Americans did.

An FSA allows employees to set aside a certain amount of their earnings into a non-taxable account for the purpose of paying for out-of-pocket medical expenses. This was advantageous for employers who didn't have to pay employment taxes on the money, and for workers who would get the income on a before-tax basis. Most used these accounts as envisioned, but some found they could afford to dump money in the accounts for scheduled medical procedures, including elective care.

For example, if a family member would be getting braces next year, the entire cost could be thrown into an FSA and used to leverage the tax laws, often gaining a substantial savings. Families with tighter budgets could have done the same but usually weren't able to free up the large sums involved.

To plug what was seen as a loophole, the ACA limits the amount that can be put in an FSA to $2,500. Amounts over this will have to be taken as regular income, subject to the normal taxes. Since this limit shifts money that would be tax-free into a taxable status, it ends up increasing tax revenue an estimated $13 billion over the life of the ACA.

CADILLAC PLANS

A new tax penalty, designed with the wealthy in mind, will attach to so-called "Cadillac" health plans. These are health insurance plans with very high coverage and no, or extremely low, co-pays. The plans are expensive, but they allow policyholders to avoid having to meet deductibles or pay cash for services.

Some Cadillac policies are offered as incentives to company executives as part of a benefits package. Others are purchased outright by those wealthy enough to afford the rates. They have been used as a way for employers to raise the level of compensation without having to pay Social Security taxes.

Under Obamacare, plans with total premiums exceeding $10,200 for individuals ($27,500 for a family) will pay a penalty of 40 percent for anything over those amounts. The penalty is levied against the insurance carrier, not the policyholder (or their employer), but the costs would probably be passed along to purchasers. This doesn't go into effect until 2018, and because insurance premiums are trending up, these plans may not be much of a "Cadillac" by the time they are taxed. With almost five years until this provision goes into effect, most do not think it will survive as written. At a minimum, the dollar amounts are likely to change. The significance of the penalty may be more political than actual—estimates on how much would be collected in 2018 and 2019 were used to show funding for the ACA and make it more palatable to fiscal conservatives.

UNINTENDED CONSEQUENCES

If Cadillac plans were solely purchased by the wealthy, the above logic would make sense. But there are a few categories of workers that will be swept up in the provisions that weren't meant to be. One is union workers. Strong unions have negotiated excellent benefit packages, including high-value health insurance.

Those with high-risk jobs would also be affected, where standard coverage, because of the abnormal risk, raises premiums. Firefighters and police officers, for example, have much higher premiums, even though they may only have normal levels of coverage. The chance that a high-risk worker will be injured or hospitalized is too great to charge them normal rates. Since the plan value is calculated on premiums, not benefits, some of these policies will be classified as Cadillacs.

Other problems come with the FSA limits. There are middle-class workers who maximize current FSA levels—not because they are trying to beat the system, but because they have a family member whose care (or the materials needed for their care) requires high out-of-pocket expenditures. These folks will be adversely affected under the ACA as well.

CHAPTER 20

Middle-Class Adults

The overall structure of Obamacare, from a funding point of view, is that impoverished Americans pay less, affluent Americans pay more, and middle-class Americans remain about the same. Unfortunately, while this is true in some circumstances, in others, middle-class families will be hit hard financially.

DEFINING MIDDLE CLASS

There's no set figure defined as middle class in the United States. The best we have is a definition of poor: the federal poverty line (FPL) that is set by the Department of Health and Human Services (HHS) and used to calculate various benefits. The average middle-class income is $50,054 (in 2012), but that doesn't tell you much about purchasing power or lifestyle. Even different government agencies disagree, with the Department of Commerce setting the income range for middle class between $50,000 and $122,000, while the Census Bureau puts it between $20,000 and $100,000.

Under the ACA, subsidies are calculated starting with the FPL and then work upward. A family that falls at or below 133 percent of the FPL will be eligible for Medicaid, essentially getting their health coverage for free. From there and up to 400 percent of the FPL, subsidies are available to help defray the cost of purchasing a policy on an insurance exchange. Using 2013 numbers, that puts an individual making $15,282 at one extreme (full ride) and someone with an income of $46,000 at the other (no subsidies). A family of four would get Medicaid if the household income is below $31,322 and lose all subsidies at $94,200.

For our purposes, middle class will start at the point where poor stops, even though this is more properly lower middle class. The range would extend up to $100,000 a year (for a family of four)—about the point where subsidies for health insurance stop.

WHY IT MATTERS

If the ACA is to remain financially neutral for middle-class adults, we need to figure out how to prevent an increase in costs to this demographic. This is the point of subsidizing health care up to the higher range of middle-class income. Subsidies are intended to neutralize the "bite" from having to purchase private insurance on your own.

Those who receive employer-sponsored insurance (ESI) will see the least impact from Obamacare. This includes middle-class adults, most of whom fall into this group. "Least impact" doesn't mean *no* impact; insurance costs still rise for this group as premiums rise. And premiums rise because the ACA sets minimums on coverage, and policies will, generally, have to cover more than they did before. More benefits translate into higher premiums. Add to this the ongoing trend of increasing health care costs, and even ESIs will demand more of the middle-class paycheck.

SELF-EMPLOYED

One segment of the middle-class demographic directly affected by Obamacare is the growing group of self-employed. These are either small business owners or freelancers—those who bear the entire cost of purchasing health care.

The ACA was drawn up with a traditional view of the middle class in mind. In this view, a single-income earner works for an employer and solely supports their family. But times have changed. The middle class is shrinking, with some moving up in income and others moving down. Many in the middle class are starting their own small businesses as a way to create and control their destiny, instead of relying on an employer.

The self-employed will have to purchase private insurance unless there is another family member who has insurance through an employer. If you are self-employed, you will be able to buy a policy for you and your family through a state insurance exchange. Exchanges are meant to combine the purchasing power of everyone who is without insurance from employment (or from Medicaid/Medicare).

Policies in the exchange will have standard benefits and premium prices, allowing for ease of comparison between companies. Private insurers will still administer the plans, but they will have to meet standards based on other offerings in your state. Practically, this means you should have access to a selection of policies at different price points, each of which are targeted to meet the needs of citizens in your state. The last condition ensures parity within a state, but what is actually covered will vary from state to state.

PROBLEMS WITH OBAMACARE FOR THE MIDDLE CLASS

The majority of the problems come from misestimating the financial burden middle-class adults will be able to bear. Those who are making ends meet without insurance will have to get a policy (or pay a penalty). Those who already have insurance will see an increase in premiums. In either case, the amount taken out of the family budget to cover health insurance will rise, and it's unknown at this point whether or not the subsidies will be enough to offset the losses in income.

So-called financially fragile families (those who are struggling, but stable in current conditions) are going to feel the squeeze. The subsidies offered anticipate this, but no one knows if the subsidies will be enough to replace income spent on health insurance. There is also the possibility that employers will drop insurance coverage, shift more of the costs to their workers, or change employment practices to increase part-time, rather than full-time positions.

A family that falls into poverty will get free coverage, but a family trying to stay afloat may find they make too much to get Medicaid but too little to afford the health insurance they had before.

One of the escape routes the ACA eliminates is the purchase of high-deductible, low-premium insurance. The "catastrophic" plan offered to those under thirty is part of the ACA, but private policies that don't meet minimum standards are not. Qualifying policies under the ACA have to cover essential health benefits (EHBs) and preventive care. Cheap policies with very poor coverage will be a thing of the past, and any available insurance will have to have the basic coverage, and the cost of this will be reflected in the premiums paid. In other words, insurance companies cannot simply remove important benefits to artificially reduce premiums.

If you decide you cannot afford even the least expensive option under Obamacare, you will be penalized when you pay your taxes. The penalty for 2014 is set at $95 per person and increases thereafter ($325 in 2015, $695 in 2016). Some will simply forego health insurance and pay the penalty. The penalties kick in for tax year 2014 and will be due when you pay your taxes in 2015.

CHAPTER 21

Impoverished Americans

One of the goals of Obamacare is to solve the problem of uninsured, poor Americans. While benefits are available under Medicaid, the so-called "working poor" commonly do not have insurance. This group consists of people and families who make too much to meet income thresholds for benefits but not enough to reasonably afford health care. But who exactly counts as impoverished depends on who you talk to.

Without health insurance, or even with policies that do not cover enough, the working poor are at risk for financial ruin if they become ill or need hospitalization. Even a short hospital stay can lead to bankruptcy or enduring debt. Hospitals are not happy with the situation either. They would prefer patients with the ability to pay, and this means either the independently wealthy or those with health insurance.

WHO COUNTS AS POOR

Because so many benefits at both the state and federal level are triggered by income, setting the proper number where subsidies begin and end becomes important, both politically and practically.

The poverty guidelines (see the tables on pages 115–116) are published by the Department of Health and Human Services (HHS) using census and other data. The guidelines are used by states and the federal government— sometimes in different ways—to determine eligibility for benefits when income is the deciding factor. The actual amounts change on an annual basis to reflect inflation and the normal costs of living most Americans have to pay.

2013 POVERTY GUIDELINES FOR THE 48 CONTIGUOUS STATES AND THE DISTRICT OF COLUMBIA

Persons in Family/Household	Poverty Guideline
For families/households with more than eight persons, add $4,020 for each additional person.	
1	$11,490
2	$15,510
3	$19,530
4	$23,550
5	$27,570
6	$31,590
7	$35,610
8	$39,630

2013 POVERTY GUIDELINES FOR ALASKA

Persons in Family/Household	Poverty Guideline
For families/households with more than eight persons, add $5,030 for each additional person.	
1	$14,350
2	$19,380
3	$24,410
4	$29,440
5	$34,470
6	$39,500
7	$44,530
8	$49,560

2013 POVERTY GUIDELINES FOR HAWAII

Persons in Family/Household	Poverty Guideline
For families/households with more than eight persons, add $4,620 for each additional person.	
1	$13,230
2	$17,850
3	$22,470
4	$27,090
5	$31,710
6	$36,330
7	$40,950
8	$45,570

Source: *Federal Register*, vol. 78, no. 16, January 24, 2013, pp. 5182–5183.

Note: Pregnant women count as two people when reading these charts.

MANDATES AND THE WORKING POOR

Under the individual mandate, every American will eventually have insurance or pay a penalty. This includes the impoverished. By requiring health insurance, the ACA seeks to solve a problem among our poor: without health insurance, they tend to use emergency room services for health conditions that could be treated less expensively through a doctor's office or clinic. They do it because emergency rooms cannot turn patients away, regardless of a person's ability to pay. By mandating coverage, Obamacare is meant to shift this burden away from overused, high-cost emergency rooms and gain an overall savings in health care costs.

Because the individual mandate forces those without insurance to obtain it, experts predict that many low-income people will apply for Medicaid, even though they have avoided it in the past. This is called the "woodwork" problem—an unknown number of qualified poor emerging from the shadows and signing up for benefits. Critics of Obamacare predict the woodwork problem will drive premiums and taxes up, as the rest of the health care system takes on the burden of this previously invisible group.

SOME STATES REBEL

Because Medicaid is paid for by both federal and state funding (matching funds), and administered by the states themselves, when Obamacare was passed, states felt they were being unduly coerced into complying with a program they didn't want. The question was whether the U.S. Congress had the power to make states follow the provisions of Obamacare and the extensions to Medicaid it included.

The matter was resolved by the U.S. Supreme Court, and a compromise position was reached. States that accepted federal funding would have to comply, except that the federal government would have to pay for any extensions to Medicaid. That is, Congress couldn't force states to participate. If a state wanted to drop the new funding, they could "opt out." This means that Obamacare for the impoverished will be different, depending on whether you live in a state that accepts the additional Medicaid funding or does not.

As of October 2013, twenty-one states have decided to opt out of the Medicaid expansion. This may change, and state legislatures are still deciding how to proceed.

WHAT TO EXPECT

There will be two tiers of subsidized health insurance for impoverished Americans. The first is simply Medicaid as it exists now, reflecting current benefits available state by state. Some services will be added, but for this tier, things stay pretty much the same.

The second level comes in those states that have opted to expand Medicaid. In those states, more Americans will qualify for Medicaid benefits. Income thresholds will be based on 133 percent of the federal poverty level (FPL). (That is the official, statutory percentage; once further refinements to the federal formula are applied, the effective figure is 138 percent. We use the more commonly cited official percentage; the two numbers produce the same criteria in absolute dollars.)

In states without Medicaid expansion (the "opt out" states), neither state nor federal subsidies will be available for those whose income is less than the subsidized Marketplace insurance threshold of 133 percent of the FPL but more than 100 percent of the FPL. Those who fall into this "Medicaid gap" will probably continue to forego or underuse needed health care services, or rely on emergency rooms for their care.

No one really knows if the threat of a tax penalty will be enough to force everyone out of the woodwork. A similar provision in Massachusetts was able to capture almost 97 percent of citizens and get them insured, but 3 to 4 percent remained off the books. It is also impossible to predict whether the newly insured under Medicaid expansion will take advantage of the services offered. Some fear they will stress the system. Others think the poor will continue to rely on emergency rooms and avoid switching to a family doctor/clinic approach.

CHAPTER 22

Uninsured Americans

The primary reason Obamacare exists is to offer a way for uninsured Americans to get health care coverage. Because of this, most of the changes have a direct impact on this segment of the population. Current estimates put the number of uninsured citizens at about 37 million. By 2019, the ACA is expected to drop this number by three-quarters, down to about 9 million. (This doesn't include people residing in the United States without legal authorization, an estimated 13 million.)

WHO ARE THE UNINSURED?

Those without health insurance in the United States fall into three broad categories: (1) those who can't afford it, (2) those who aren't sure about it, and (3) those who can't get it.

Those Who Can't Afford It

This group would purchase health insurance if they were able to, and the "affordable" in the Affordable Care Act refers mainly to this demographic. Three provisions of Obamacare directly address the cost of health insurance to make it both available and affordable to this group:

- Expanded eligibility for Medicaid would have allowed enrollment by previously excluded low-income people who earn up to 133 percent of the federal poverty level (FPL). In the wake of a Supreme Court decision making state participation optional, only twenty-five states have opted to expand Medicaid eligibility.
- Those who do not qualify for Medicaid because of income but earn up to 400 percent of the FPL will be offered subsidized health care—so long as they live in a state that chose to "opt in" to the Medicaid extension plan.
- Those who are employed may benefit from new rules and penalties imposed on employers to encourage employer-sponsored insurance.

Those Who Aren't Sure

Young and healthy adults are sometimes referred to as "invincibles," not because they really are immune to harm, but because they have a reputation as risk-takers and are thought not see a need to have health insurance, an expense cost that doesn't return any immediate benefits. According to recent research, however, the "young invincibles" overwhelmingly see the value of health insurance. Their concerns and doubts actually revolve more around whether they will be able to afford it.

Getting this group on the insurance rolls is an important part of the overall economic future of Obamacare. Because the young are relatively healthy, they end up being net payers instead of consumers of health care, and their contributions help support other groups that use the medical system more. Of course, some of the "invincibles" do get ill or hurt. In that case, having an active insurance policy will allow them to use the appropriate medical services instead of relying on emergency rooms for their care. This helps reduce costs as well.

Current efforts to enroll young and healthy Americans focus on acknowledging that they have yet to reach their full earnings potential, and stress the federal help that is available to make insurance affordable.

Those Who Can't Get It

Those in the United States without legal authorization receive no benefits from Obamacare and pay no penalties. In a sense, they are invisible to the ACA. Some may be able to afford private insurance, but benefits through an insurance exchange or Medicaid are denied under ACA or state policies.

Others, who have been denied coverage based on a medical condition, will be able to pick up some type of policy. Although coverage cannot be denied for a preexisting condition, the type and price of the policy offered depends on state-level rules and whether patients qualify for other benefits, like disability under Social Security. Charitable organizations will still have a role to play in filling payment gaps.

The biggest group of those who can't get insurance despite being legally entitled to it under Obamacare are residents of states who still have not accepted Medicaid expansion. Their lack of options remains much as it was before, at least until the political wrangling ends—or they move to a participating state.

THE PENALTIES

Many of the uninsured will take advantage of policies offered through a health exchange, but some may decide to forego getting insurance and simply pay the tax penalty. If you choose to pay the tax instead, you will initially be hit with a $95 fee or 1 percent of your income, whichever is greater. The fee for 2014 tops out at $285.

The fees go up for 2015 and 2016, and will be adjusted based on cost-of-living numbers thereafter. If you don't pay the penalty, the IRS will seize what it needs from any refund due to you. Failing that, they will send you threatening letters about it. There is currently no mechanism to make it a criminal offense and they cannot put a tax lien on your property because you didn't pay the penalty.

All in all, the penalties are designed to be painful enough to move the uninsured over to the insured side of the ledger, and if not, to still collect what they would otherwise have contributed to fund Obamacare.

WHAT ABOUT EXEMPTIONS?

There are very few complete exemptions from Obamacare. Even those temporary exemptions that did exist will expire (or have already). A few remain, and only a very few of those allow someone to remain uninsured.

The most used permanent exemption is likely to be for religious reasons. Certain religious groups have a long history of not participating in Social Security or similar programs, neither paying into nor accepting benefits from such programs. The Amish are a good example, and this religious tradition has a long history of self-sufficiency.

Any individual may apply for an exemption on religious or other grounds, but such an application is likely to fail unless they can demonstrate adherence to a religious philosophy that forbids participation and one that has been in continuous existence since the 1950s. So a modern Wiccan is unlikely to qualify. There's one other catch, too: if you manage to get an exemption from Obamacare, you'll also end up exempt from Social Security at the same time.

The only other category of exemption exists for those in the United States as students or workers for foreign nationals. They are not citizens and not subject to Social Security or Medicare taxes.

Exemptions for public workers or union employees depend on having an equivalent system in place (equivalent to Social Security and Medicare) and people in this category would be considered insured.

For the vast majority of the uninsured, the bottom line is clear: get insured.

CHAPTER 23

People with Mental Illness and Developmental Disabilities

Current statistics state that about one in four Americans currently has a diagnosable mental illness, including behavioral illnesses like substance use disorders. And with the publication of the latest edition of the *Diagnostic Services Manual* (the "bible" used by mental health professionals), even more diagnostic categories have been created.

Before Obamacare, it was apparent that many who should be getting mental health services were not. Sometimes this was because these disorders were seen as shameful and people avoided treatment, but other times it really was a funding issue. Publically funded mental health services have chronically been underfunded—an easy place to cut services when state revenues fall short. The ACA tries to remedy this by adding new benefits, both to Medicaid and under the essential health benefits (EHB) section of the act.

MEDICAID EXPANSION

Early expansion of services, including mental health treatment, has already happened. By 2013, offering more mental health services under Medicaid showed an upward trend in use. This early expansion targeted lower-income patients, who have a larger proportion of mental illness and substance abuse.

(Many conditions are linked to poverty risk.) In 2014, the Medicaid expansion to those making up to 133 percent of the federal poverty line (FPL) starts. But this next group isn't expected to need as many services on a per capita basis.

One of the expanded coverages allows patients to access Medicaid without having to meet strict disability guidelines. This puts mental illness on par with physical illness when deciding whether or not a patient is capable of holding down a job.

On the flip side, with more money available to pay for services, hospitals and clinics are scrambling to meet the needs of these new patients. In some states, mental health services have been inadequate and they are playing catch-up to meet the increased demand.

Changes in Medicare also figure into the mix. By closing the "donut hole" in prescription coverage, it is likely that seniors will be able to afford the psychiatric medications they need, which are often expensive and available only as brand-name drugs.

PRIVATE INSURANCE

Because mental health care is considered an essential benefit, all qualifying policies will now have some form of coverage. This coverage may be deemed an essential preventive measure (such as screening for depression) and fully covered with no co-pay or fee. But most services will be handled in the same manner as any other disease condition. In fact, the ACA includes language stating that mental health care has to be handled the same way as other benefits.

An insurer is not allowed to ban someone with a mental illness as a pre-existing condition. They must offer hospitalization, outpatient treatment, and prescription drug benefits on par with whatever they offer for other disease conditions.

OTHER PROVISIONS

Obamacare provides funding for innovative new mental health treatments and therapies. Prevention is promoted, along with shifting patients to home and community-centered care, instead of using the institutional mechanism as the default. Substance abuse services are specifically mentioned, and counseling for addiction is built into the essential services under Obamacare.

These free services are provided by primary-care doctors, an important innovation. Many families complain that it took months or years to get a diagnosis and treatment for a loved one with a mental illness. By putting some screening services right in the family doctor's office, these gatekeepers can now act to catch conditions early and make referrals to mental health specialists. The idea is to move services closer to the general population, instead of keeping mental health as a special category, separate from other health services. If the idea works, more people will get diagnosed, get diagnosed earlier, and receive care without having to overcome so many hurdles.

A FLY IN THE OINTMENT

As laid out, the outlook is good for those with mental illness. But there are likely to be some serious problems to overcome. We've already mentioned one: the lack of resources to meet this newly funded need. There are a few others as well.

Because EHBs vary—within federally set minimums—from state to state, the services actually offered, and how much they cost, will also vary. The general rule, for private insurance (or insurance purchased through a government-run insurance exchange) is that minimum coverage will be set based on the largest small-group policy already offered in the state. This means the responsible parties will look around and see what's being offered, at what price, and then decide what coverage will be like in that state for mental health services. Existing or evolving state regulations on mental health coverage may also make for some variations.

Some services will have to be offered based on national standards. For example, a typical plan will pay for 95 percent of both inpatient and outpatient mental health care. The problem, however, is setting a premium rate for this benefit. In states where mental health services are very expensive, it will be impossible to offer coverage at the same low rate enjoyed by policyholders in other states with lower cost-of-living rates.

A second problem is one shared by Obamacare overall: Will the funding meet the need? Mental health services, especially those that require chronic treatment, are expensive. If it is accepted that many mental illnesses are not curable, but merely controllable, that requires a lifetime commitment and lifetime funding as well.

There was a reason insurance companies tried to drop mental health coverage. If people suffering from mental illness represent a burden not covered by premiums, they become a net loss. In a partially public-funded system, those losses have to be balanced out. No one knows if this will be the case. Obamacare skeptics point to increased mental health services as one area that can bankrupt the entire program.

What mental health patients actually see on the ground (and pay for) will change in response to these issues as well as to how well the overall economy is doing. Like other aspects of the ACA, a robust economy generates more taxes and eases the funding burden. A sluggish economy does the opposite.

CHAPTER 24

Immigrants

Like many other provisions under U.S. law, immigration status will determine how Obamacare affects a particular individual. In most cases, an immigrant residing in the United States legally will be treated as a citizen would, while those here without legal authorization will not be.

UNDOCUMENTED IMMIGRANTS

Largely invisible to the health care system, undocumented immigrants are neither covered nor penalized under the ACA. Their situation will continue as before, with most getting services through emergency rooms, where they cannot be denied care. Others will use clinics and pay cash for health care. Where possible, those who are seriously ill may return to their country of origin and get care there.

Undocumented immigrants are also excluded from purchasing health care through the insurance exchanges, although they will still be able to buy private health insurance or get insurance through an employer. Those who are here illegally are also not subject to the tax penalties under Obamacare.

After Obamacare is fully up and running, undocumented immigrants will represent the largest group of uninsured in America. This will happen automatically as other groups are absorbed into the system. These immigrants will remain behind while others get on the insurance rolls.

IMMIGRANTS AWAITING CITIZENSHIP

Those who are have legal permission to reside in the United States but who are not yet full citizens are subject to the ACA, with some modifications. For example, although these noncitizen residents are eligible to use the insurance exchanges, they may not yet be eligible for Medicaid.

Even when income levels would otherwise allow Medicaid benefits, those with legal permission to reside in the United States still have to wait five years before an application will be accepted. Under these circumstances, subsidies will be provided. The subsidy is used to defray the cost of a policy from the exchange and is calculated based on income. The net effect is that, even though ineligible for Medicaid, a person may obtain the same coverage at low cost or no cost through a subsidy.

Legal immigrants also face the same tax penalties if they choose not to get health insurance. In general, besides the Medicaid exception, immigrants awaiting citizenship are treated exactly the same as citizens under the ACA.

Please refer to other sections in this book that apply to you to find out the details that vary based on age, income, and employment status. These factors will have more of an impact than citizenship status for noncitizen residents.

IMMIGRATION REFORM

Legislation to provide a path to citizenship for undocumented immigrants has been introduced, and as of 2013, is being debated in Congress. Although the final form of any such legislation is unknown, it will almost certainly include a kind of "in-between" status. This happens when someone starts out as an illegal immigrant but is working toward a status change. The in-between status can extend for a decade or more before residency or citizenship is obtained.

At this time, the legislation exempts undocumented immigrants who are working toward obtaining citizenship, allowing them to work in the United States but not requiring them to meet the individual mandate under Obamacare.

If this version of immigration reform passes, it may create an unintended class of worker: one who is authorized to work but who will not subject an employer to the penalties under the ACA. Such a worker would be very attractive to a business wishing to increase staff without going over the fifty-employee ceiling that triggers some of the onerous requirements of Obamacare. Should this happen, the "in-between" worker may be in demand, over and above a citizen with the same qualifications.

OTHER CIRCUMSTANCES

In many cases, an immigrant is not here alone; they are often the spouse or dependent of someone who is a citizen or resident alien. Someone who is part of a family may be eligible for coverage under another family member's plan, either through employment or directly from a private insurer. Insurance products don't automatically discriminate based on citizenship status, although government-funded policies will.

Those who are in the United States under a visa are also not subject to the provisions of Obamacare. The act includes the following language:

> "Access limited to lawful residents. If an individual is not, or is not reasonably expected to be for the entire period for which enrollment is sought, a citizen or national of the United States or an alien lawfully present in the United States, the individual shall not be treated as a qualified individual and may not be covered under a qualified health plan in the individual market that is offered through an Exchange."

Immigration matters are complex and the consequences of making an error can be severe. For this reason, it would be wise to seek a valid legal opinion before deciding whether your immigration status meets all, some, or none of the rules under Obamacare. This book is not meant to be taken as legal advice. Only a qualified attorney can counsel you on the legal issues surrounding your immigration status.

CHAPTER 25

Small Business Owners

A small business is defined under the ACA as having fifty employees or fewer. Part-time workers are counted based on the number of hours worked a month. Every 120 hours of part-time wages paid per month counts as one full-time worker. This prevents employers from avoiding the rules by hiring only part-time help.

WHY SMALL AND LARGE?

When the ACA was being debated, one concern was the difference in financial burdens small and large companies would face with standardized insurance coverage. Larger businesses have economies of scale and power in the marketplace that smaller businesses do not. IBM can negotiate to get lower health insurance rates for its employees, and because they consolidate administrative costs, managing health insurance for their employees is also less expensive.

Before the ACA, the result of the disparity in costs was already evident. Among larger businesses (more than one hundred employees), employer-sponsored insurance (ESI) was the rule—76 percent offered it. At the same time, small businesses were running at about 37 percent. New reporting requirements under Obamacare add even more of an administrative burden than before.

To offset this, small businesses are treated differently and not bound by the same rules as large businesses.

EMPLOYER MANDATE FOR SMALL BUSINESSES

To gain the economies of scale large businesses enjoy, the ACA provides for consolidating purchases of insurance through exchanges. The Small Business Health Options Program (SHOP) will be set up by states and include policies with the minimum coverage Obamacare requires.

As envisioned, a statewide risk pool would lower costs to small businesses, allowing them to leverage group buying power. The Congressional Budget Office estimates that two million Americans would access health insurance through small business employment under the SHOP program.

Small businesses do not have to purchase insurance for their employees. However, there may be significant tax advantages for doing so.

Very small businesses (twenty-five or fewer employees) are also eligible for tax credits to help pay for coverage through SHOP. To receive the credit, these companies would have to pay 50 percent of their employees' insurance costs, and employees can make no more than $50,000 per year in wages. These tax credits are scaled by company size and wage rates, with the largest going to companies with fewer than ten workers and wages at $25,000 or less. Credits go as high as 50 percent of an employer's contribution to health insurance.

The credits disappear after 2015, when SHOP is supposed to be fully functional.

THE 50TH EMPLOYEE DILEMMA

Since the defining characteristic for a small business is fewer than fifty employees (full-time equivalents, or FTEs), companies should be aware of when they cross that line and what it will mean. The mandates are different for large businesses and the penalties for noncompliance more severe.

To avoid crossing the line, several strategies have been suggested. One is to outsource work to subcontractors who are not counted as employees. This is popular when staffing needs can be met through online freelancers or by hiring temp workers. Another is to move past the fifty-worker total, but do it with more part-time help. Although the provisions would still kick in, part-time workers do not have to be offered health insurance, as long as they don't exceed thirty hours a week.

Some small businesses will face difficult decisions, especially when their profits depend directly on the number of workers. A classic example would be a temp agency—the more people they get out working, the more the agency makes. Under the old system, temps would be encouraged to work as many hours as possible, but now, it might be advantageous to limit them to less than thirty hours a week. Further, taking on new temp workers to contract out can't be done without limit. At some point, even for a temp agency with a small office and a couple of phones, they cross the line and become a "large business."

The bright dividing line between fifty and fifty-one employees is considered a defect in Obamacare. Pundits argue that a sliding scale is more realistic, although they agree it is also more complicated. Still, as of the middle of 2013, more small businesses than ever before have decided to provide health insurance. It remains to be seen if the trend will continue.

OUTSIDE FORCES

When unemployment is high and wages are low, small businesses find they can cut back on health insurance as a benefit and still get the workers they need. If the economy improves and labor becomes harder to come by, most of the preceding considerations will not apply. Small businesses will want to offer ESI as an incentive. But even if they don't offer it, higher wages will fill the same purpose because employees will be able to buy a policy themselves to meet the individual mandate requirements.

Perhaps the greatest outside force impacting Obamacare and small businesses is not the economic landscape but the political one. As of late September 2013, small business owners could still get substantial tax credits for buying employee insurance from private brokers, but the promised SHOP Marketplace was delayed a month, and offered much less than had been promised—highlighting small business vulnerability at the hands of government bureaucrats. In October 2013, House Republicans, pushed by members of the Tea Party, attempted to tie funding for the government to defunding or delaying Obamacare. As a result, the vote to pass the spending bill was delayed, and for the first time in seventeen years the government was shut down. The shutdown of the federal government demonstrated the strength of entrenched political opposition that could eventually bring a radical overhaul of Obamacare, should control of the White House and Congress shift through the electoral process.

The uncertainty is palpable. It makes long-term planning difficult. In this environment, small businesses have an advantage (the same advantage they always have): the ability to act quickly when conditions shift.

CHAPTER 26

Large Business Owners

Mandates under Obamacare for businesses are more restrictive if a company employs more than fifty workers. This is the dividing line between small and large businesses. The number is calculated based on full-time workers or what is known as the *full-time equivalent* (FTE). Every 120 hours per month paid to part-time workers counts as one full-time worker when calculating small versus large. A part-time worker is defined as someone who works thirty or fewer hours a week.

EMPLOYER MANDATES

The ACA doesn't directly legislate what large businesses have to do for health insurance. It is a myth that employers must offer insurance, and a company can choose to offer no health care at all. Instead, Obamacare imposes penalties on large employers to incentivize offering health insurance to their workers.

Since most private insurance (as contrasted with Medicare and Medicaid) is obtained through employers, the ACA attempts to influence the type of insurance, without being so onerous that employers decide to drop the benefit altogether.

The "mandate" refers to what employers have to offer their employees if they choose to offer insurance at all. For large employers, this is less likely to cause problems, unless the nature of the business is to pay wages at the lower end of the pay scale. This is because the penalties for not offering insurance kick in only when at least one full-time employee qualifies for a government insurance subsidy. If everyone in the company is making more than 400 percent of the federal poverty line (FPL) (calculated for the family, not just the employee), there is no problem—the mandate under Obamacare is on the individual to get insurance, not on the employer to provide it.

Employers who have at least one person who qualifies for subsidized insurance and who do not offer a health insurance benefit will be penalized. But even then, the penalty may be less than it would cost to offer an insurance benefit. This fact spawned a great deal of worry about employers simply dropping current plans and paying the penalty instead. So far, it hasn't happened.

WHAT PLANS QUALIFY?

Since most large businesses already have an insurance benefit, the general practice will be to make sure policies are "ACA compliant" and otherwise continue on as before. So long as certain guidelines are met, an employer-sponsored insurance (ESI) policy can be kept in place.

Some of the key guidelines large businesses will have to meet to avoid penalties include the following:

- Policies must pay for the same basic care (EHBs, or essential health benefits) as policies in state insurance exchanges. This provision keeps insurers from selling plans that have artificially low premiums because of lowered benefits. There is a "floor" in play.
- Employees cannot be charged more than 9.5 percent of their wages to cover premiums. In some cases, this means benefits will have to be reduced to keep premiums beneath this target, especially for lower-wage workers.

- There are limits on deductibles and out-of-pocket costs. Health savings accounts are also capped.
- Plans offered must have an actuarial value of at least 60 percent. This means that, on average, the policy covers 60 percent of the medical costs of a policyholder. This mirrors what will be offered in insurance exchanges, and higher-value policies are allowed.

THE FREE RIDER PENALTY

All Americans will be able to access private health insurance through a state-level insurance exchange, and many of those will get a subsidy from the government to help pay premiums. The subsidy represents "free" money and may result in abuse. To deal with this, Obamacare includes a "free rider" penalty; however, the penalty is on the employer, not the individual who is being subsidized.

It works this way: if any full-time employee qualifies for a subsidy and their employer doesn't offer a qualifying policy, then the employer must pay a penalty, not just for that worker, but for every employee over the age of thirty.

This is meant to keep employers from dropping insurance and having their employees access subsidized insurance instead—essentially a free ride. The penalty is supposed to make up the difference. In effect, employers who foist off health care onto taxpayers (by way of subsidies) will have to pay more in taxes. (The penalties are administered as taxes instead of fines, a legal nuance allowing federal intrusion into the process.)

The free rider penalty is calculated in one of two ways. The first uses the total number of employees minus thirty, times $2,000. So, for example, a company that has sixty full-time employees and is subject to the penalty, would have a tax burden of 60 – 30 × $2,000 = $60,000.

The second is a straight penalty of $3,000 per worker for only those workers eligible for subsidies. Employers pay the lesser of these two penalties.

ACCESS TO EXCHANGES

Large businesses are not allowed to shop on the insurance exchanges, at least not until 2017. This is because they already have the muscle to negotiate insurance rates with private carriers and because the law was written with a nod to insurance companies already servicing this part of the market.

The expectation is that strong competition in insurance exchanges will drive prices lower, making health exchange policies a better deal for many who receive employer-sponsored insurance now. The consequences may be a shift away from employment-based health insurance to individual, exchange-based insurance. If this happens, even large employers will lose their ability to shape the market, and the advantage of scale will disappear.

HOW WILL MY BUSINESS BE AFFECTED?

Most large businesses will see little change, although employees will likely see an increase in premiums as additional, mandated coverage is added. Premium increases have continued to be the rule, even without Obamacare, and this feeds into the higher premiums as well.

Businesses that are flirting with the fifty-employee cutoff may have to consider hiring practices. In some cases, it will make sense to create more part-time positions instead of adding full-timers. Subcontracting and outsourcing are also made more attractive as both of these types of workers do not count toward the total number of employees.

Wages will have to be considered in light of health care. A business will have to be careful about offering policies that burden employees beyond the 9.5 percent level. Wages also matter when an employee doesn't make enough to keep them out of the subsidy pool, as the free rider provision may kick in.

CHAPTER 27

Pharmaceutical Companies

At first glance, it's a bit of a surprise that the pharmaceutical industry supported the ACA. After all, the new rules would give tremendous negotiating power to large insurance entities, and this power has been used in the past to chip away at profit margins. But Big Pharma supported the legislation, and there's a simple, logical chain that explains it.

The drug industry depends on doctors to write prescriptions. Doctors write prescriptions only for patients under their care, so increasing the public's contact with health professionals is one way to increase sales of prescription drugs. A second phenomenon is in play as well: those with drug coverage are much more likely to get a prescription filled than those who have to pay the full costs. It's no different than accessing any other area of health care—the more someone has to pay out of pocket, the less likely they are to seek treatment.

HOLDING DOWN THE COSTS OF PRESCRIPTION DRUGS

One of the key provisions in Obamacare is directed at controlling rising drug costs. For Medicare patients, the drug companies are even contributing directly, offering a 50 percent discount to Medicare patients to help close the "donut hole" (a gap in coverage many seniors face when drug costs go above a $2,800 ceiling).

In some countries, the price of pharmaceuticals is regulated by the government. This is not the case in the United States, but the threat of doing so is usually enough to make Big Pharma capitulate on other price-containment options. By offering what amounts to a huge cut in profits from Medicare patients, the pharmaceutical industry will gain access to as many as 19 million new enrollees in Medicaid as well as individuals who will have to get private insurance under Obamacare.

Forbes reported that the net result is an expected $115 billion in new business over the next decade. This surprising outcome relies on a basic economic principle—getting a smaller profit from a hugely increased customer base generates more profits in the end. With about 10 percent of the health care market going to prescription drugs, there's money to be made.

It's not one-sided, though. Medicaid rebates, formularies that push generics, and a watchful eye on price increases mean pharmaceutical companies can't simply charge whatever they feel like—except in one growing sector or the market: small-group products. These are drugs that treat specific conditions in a relatively small pool of patients with certain conditions. Specific cancers are one example, but AIDS was probably the first. Drug companies found they could charge high prices when they had little or no competition. This is now seen as a growth area: expensive medicines that serve a small population.

AMERICANS LOVE PILLS

Have you ever wondered why television advertisements for prescription drugs fill the airwaves even though viewers cannot purchase the items without a prescription? It seems silly to push products the public can't buy. But it turns out that many patients are perfectly willing to pressure their doctors into trying something they've seen on television or in a magazine advertisement.

In many ways, the practice of medicine has become a matter of matching a disease and a patient to some combination of pills. Very few doctors would risk not prescribing something, even when they do not have full confidence in the prescription they write. In many cases, they are using a "we'll see what happens" logic, prescribing a best guess and then reevaluating the situation at a follow-up appointment.

Almost half of all Americans take some prescription drug. We average four prescriptions per person overall. Unlike other forms of health care, even the young and relatively healthy are reached by our drug habit, with birth control, pain medications, and antibiotics being popular with young adults.

FEEDING THE TREND

An additional driver of business for the pharmaceutical companies is the rising costs of health care elsewhere in the system. The amount Americans spend on pharmaceuticals trends upward, but it's running at about only a 2 percent increase per year. That's less than other parts of the medical system.

The net result is that, overall, money is saved by treating patients on an outpatient basis with a prescription instead of using office visits or inpatient care. This also serves as a way to move patients out of hospitals early. It is not uncommon for patients to receive home care, including IVs, when they stabilize enough to be moved out of a hospital bed.

There's another surprising twist. Just as clinics and hospitals are trying to get patients out the door, pharmacy chains are looking to get those same people through *their* doors. By offering new services that used to require a clinic visit, Walgreens, CVS, Walmart, and other chains are increasing their business. The services are generally high profit and low resource. Vaccinations are common, but chains also may hire a nurse practitioner to offer blood pressure screenings and other services paid for under Obamacare.

CHAPTER 28

Insurance Companies Under Obamacare

Insurance companies have been scrambling to both understand and meet their new obligations under Obamacare. Several changes have already taken effect and there are more coming. The changes primarily come through regulating minimum coverage allowed and by standardizing policies. The purposes are twofold. Minimal coverage through essential health benefits (EHBs) is supposed to increase access to preventive health care and gain ground in overall public health. A second, related purpose is to make health insurance more transparent through the standardization of policies under four general levels: Platinum, Gold, Silver, and Bronze.

ESSENTIAL HEALTH BENEFITS

One way private insurance companies have traditionally competed is by matching benefits to policyholder needs. Lower costs can be offered with fewer covered benefits or through higher deductibles or co-pays. Following a "you get what you pay for" model, this practice has led to a phenomenal number of different, customized policies across the nation. A particular carrier will sometimes offer a hundred or more different plans, sometimes with a dozen choices for employees of the same company.

EHBs carve out a set of services that all insurance plans must offer, setting a "floor" on coverage. Doing this means that some services won't be used by policyholders who are the wrong sex or age or don't have certain conditions (like diabetes or high blood pressure). Males, for instance, participate in the same plan that covers breast exams and pregnancy services.

However, by regulating insurance companies in this way, the ACA puts an emphasis on preventive care services that have been shown to reduce costs to the entire system in the long-term. It's as simple as detecting a health need early enough to treat it less expensively or preventing a communicable disease from spreading by giving free vaccinations. Essential health benefits fall into one of the following ten categories:

- Ambulatory patient services, such as doctor visits and outpatient services
- Emergency services
- Hospitalization
- Maternity and newborn care
- Mental health and substance use disorder services, including behavioral health treatment
- Prescription drugs
- Rehabilitative and habilitative services and devices
- Laboratory services
- Preventive and wellness services and chronic disease management
- Pediatric services, including oral and vision care

These benefits are meant to match up with best practices and policies already offered by many carriers, but with one caveat: patients cannot be charged a co-pay or deductible for the covered items.

WHO DECIDES?

Under the ACA, the secretary of Health and Human Services sets the scope of the EHBs. This puts the federal government directly in the mix, but only has practical consequences when an EHB requires more than what an insurance policy would already cover. Those policies that already offer more than the new minimums won't change.

Insurers are allowed to increase premiums when benefits increase under the EHB standard. But they can't do it without showing increased costs. And if they end up charging too much, based on inflated estimates, overages must be refunded to policyholders.

Insurers are also bound by state-level regulations. This means they have to meet the higher of two standards—either the EHB services under Obamacare or whatever is mandated by the state they operate in, with an important nuance. States that mandate higher standards than the ACA will have to pay the difference between premium costs. So, for example, if Texas requires policies to cover plastic surgery (a fictional example), and the ACA does not, then Texas would have to pay the difference in the premium cost to add this benefit. Policyholders would not have to pay an increased premium just because Texas requires plastic surgery care when Obamacare does not.

This rule applies only to a state mandate. When no mandate is in place, policies can be offered with plastic surgery (or any other coverage) if policyholders are willing to pay for it.

INSURANCE EXCHANGES

While EHB and the mandates cover all policies offered, Obamacare also creates insurance exchanges. This provides a virtual marketplace where consumers can compare prices among similar policies. Other plans can be offered outside of the insurance exchange, but in order to compete in an exchange, an insurer has to structure a policy along certain guidelines. There are four levels of policies:

* Platinum: 90 percent covered, 10 percent deductible
* Gold: 80 percent covered, 20 percent deductible

- Silver: 70 percent covered, 30 percent deductible
- Bronze: 60 percent covered, 40 percent deductible

These percentages are based on what is known as "actuarial value." The value of a plan is determined by what the average patient would be expected to pay, based on the average level of medical care they receive. And just as with traditional policies, the more coverage someone gets, the higher the premium they pay.

How much a person actually pays in deductibles depends on which health care services they use. If they stick to only benefits covered under EHB that come with no out-of-pocket fees, or if they don't use the medical system at all, they won't pay anything.

Using these definitions, it is expected that those who use less health care will gravitate to the Silver or Bronze plans, which feature a lower premium and higher out-of-pocket costs, while those who need more services will pay higher premiums and get a Platinum or Gold plan. If this happens, the higher-tier plans will attract more of the sick among the population, and premiums for these plans will increase to meet the higher demand.

It's important to note that insurers aren't necessarily going to lose money with any of these changes. Premiums will rise, depending on whether costs rise. What is different, though, is that insurers cannot unilaterally raise rates; they have to justify increases based on provable costs.

One final nuance is that insurers are not allowed to increase deductibles beyond a regulated amount. At some point, even the lowest-ranked plan (Bronze plan) will reach this limit, and costs above that amount will be borne entirely by the policy. This mechanism is meant to help stop the financial ruin patients face when they are unable to pay for medical care. The limits recently changed, but in 2012, they were set at $6,000 for individuals and $12,000 for families on exchange-type policies. Limits were set lower for small business–funded policies.

PATIENT PROTECTION AND OTHER CHANGES

Barring someone for a preexisting condition or dropping coverage because of a disease condition is no longer allowed under Obamacare. Lifetime coverage limits will be prohibited starting in 2014, meaning a carrier cannot drop a patient with a chronic disease when they exceed a certain amount of care.

Rescissions are not allowed under Obamacare. These refer to a practice insurance companies use to deny coverage when errors were detected in policy applications. For example, if a woman didn't know she was pregnant when signing up for a policy, and then tried to get maternity benefits a few months later, the insurer might rescind the policy. The grounds for rescission in this case would be an allegation of fraud, since the woman didn't declare her pregnancy as a preexisting condition. The practice was sometimes abused, and insurers would use any error they could find to cancel a policy if it appeared a large claim would be made. (This is now illegal.)

Children and young people under twenty-six years old will have to be offered coverage under a parent's policy, even if the child doesn't live at home, is married, is otherwise not a dependent, or even if the young person is eligible for insurance with an employer.

Glossary

This section includes terms used in this book as well as general terms used by the insurance industry, the Department of Health and Human Services, and the Department of Labor when discussing the ACA.

ACA. See Affordable Care Act, a shortened form of Patient Protection and Affordable Care Act (PPACA).

Actuarial Value. The value of an insurance policy based on its average benefit to the consumer over a broad pool of enrollees. The minimum actuarial value allowed under Obamacare is 60 percent, meaning that, on average, policyholders will pay 40 percent of all health care costs with this policy. Higher actuarial values are allowed, where policyholders pay less than 40 percent.

Affordable Care Act. The 2010 legislation and amendments that created Obamacare. Sometimes used synonymously with "Obamacare."

Allowed Amount. Maximum payment authorized for covered health services, devices, or prescriptions. A charge above this amount will have to be paid by the patient.

Appeal. A formal request for an insurer to review a decision.

Balance Billing. The process when an insurer bills a policyholder for the difference between the allowed amount and the amount charged by a provider. Some providers are restricted and cannot bill for more than the allowed amount.

Cadillac Plan. An insurance plan with high premiums and high benefits, low deductibles, and low out-of-pocket costs.

Co-insurance. The amount patients pay for health services after their deductible is met, calculated as a percentage.

Common Control. A provision in the ACA that prevents a company from splitting up to avoid having more than 50 employees in the same business. Multiple entities that are directed centrally (common control) are treated as one business under the ACA rules.

Co-payment (or **co-pay**). A fixed amount patients pay whenever they access a category of care. For example, prescription coverage may have a $10 co-pay that must be paid for each prescription.

Deductible. The amount patients pay before insurance coverage starts. This is paid first, and when met, only then does insurance start to pick up some of the costs.

Department of Health and Human Services. The U.S. government's principal agency for protecting the health of all Americans and providing essential human services, especially for those who are least able to help themselves.

Dependent. Under Obamacare, the status of any child under twenty-six years old, regardless of financial dependence or whether or not they appear as a dependent on tax forms.

DME. See durable medical equipment.

Durable Medical Equipment. Medical devices that are used in ongoing care, such as a wheelchair or diabetic testing supplies.

Employer Mandate. The penalties employers pay if they do not offer a qualified policy to their employees.

Employer-Sponsored Insurance. Health insurance offered through an employer who pays some or all of the premium costs.

ESI. See employer-sponsored insurance.

Excluded Services. Health care services that are not covered by a policy and may be specifically identified as such.

Federal Poverty Line. A dollar figure published by the Department of Health and Human Services (HHS) that sets an income-based definition for poverty in the United States. The actual number is updated annually and depends on the number of family members in a household.

Flexible Spending Account. A tax-deferred account; it includes health savings accounts as a subtype.

FPL. See federal poverty line (also, federal poverty level).

Free Riders. Those who do not have health insurance and who use hospital emergency services without paying. Large employers are penalized for creating free riders among their employees by not offering adequate health insurance.

FSA. See flexible spending account.

FTE. See full-time equivalent (also, full-time employee).

Full-Time Equivalent. A combination of part-time workers whose hours total thirty hours a week (or averages 120 hours a month). For every combination that totals thirty hours a week (or 120 hours in a month), a full-time equivalent is used when calculating the number of full-time employees in a business.

Grievance. A formal complaint to an insurer, usually related to an appeal when care is denied.

Habilitation Services. Health care or therapy designed to aid patients in meeting the demands of their daily lives. Usually a mix of inpatient and outpatient services.

Health Insurance Marketplace. Sometimes known as health insurance exchange (HIX) or Marketplace. A virtual marketplace set up at the state level, or sometimes run by the federal government, where private insurance companies can compete for business from those authorized to use the exchange.

Health Savings Account. A type of FSA that allows employees to get tax-free money for use as payment for health care expenses.

HHS. See Department of Health and Human Services.

HIX. Health insurance exchange; see health insurance marketplace.

HSA. See health savings account.

Independent Payment Advisory Board. A board created by the ACA to advise on Medicare payment cuts or alterations independently of Congress or the executive branch.

Individual Mandate. The requirement, enforced by tax penalties, for individuals to obtain a qualified health insurance policy.

In-network. Services rendered as part of a health care contract between a provider and an insurance company. Co-pays and co-insurance are usually lower for in-network care.

IPAB. See Independent Payment Advisory Board.

Large Employer. A business with more than fifty full-time or full-time equivalent employees.

Look-Back. A rule used when calculating whether an employee should be counted as full- or part-time. If a worker has logged an average of thirty hours per week over a three month period (the look-back) they will be counted as full-time, even if they work less than thirty hours currently.

Medically Necessary. Health services that meet current standards of care to treat, diagnose, or prevent recognized medical conditions. Treatments that are not medically necessary will usually not be covered by insurance.

Minimum Value. The actuarial value of a health insurance plan, calculated as a percentage of the health costs it pays. Minimum value is used to stratify Marketplace plans into Platinum (90 percent of costs covered) to Bronze (60 percent of costs covered). Employee-sponsored plans must meet Marketplace minimum value or generate penalties. Some state and federal benchmarks are based on a Silver plan (minimum actuarial value of 70 percent).

Obamacare. The umbrella term for the ACA, its amendments, and all the regulations that flow from it, including changes to Medicare and Medicaid. Sometimes used synonymously with ACA.

Out-of-Network. Services rendered by providers who have not contracted with your insurance company and where you will usually pay more as a co-pay or co-insurance.

Out-of-Pocket. Fees paid directly by patients to providers, but these may be billed through an insurance plan for accounting purposes.

Out-of-Pocket Limit. An annual limit in expenses that patients pay for covered services. Once reached, any further allowed amounts will be paid by the insurance itself (usually excluding any co-pays).

Participating Provider. A medical service provider (doctor or institution) that contracts with your insurance company to offer care at a discounted price. You may pay less if you use a participating provider, but more than that if you see a preferred provider; see Preferred Provider.

Patient Protection and Affordable Care Act. See Affordable Care Act.

Play or Pay. The policy of charging employers who do not offer health care to their employees. Companies who do not offer health plans (play) will be penalized with higher taxes (pay).

PPACA. Patient Protection and Affordable Care Act (see Affordable Care Act).

Preauthorization. Also called prior approval or prior authorization, this is a specific ruling by an insurance company that a procedure or service or medical device is medically necessary. It doesn't automatically mean they will cover all, or any, of the cost.

Preferred Provider. A medical service provider who contracts with your insurance company and offers the lowest rates for covered services. You may pay a lower co-pay or co-insurance if you see a preferred provider. See In-Network and Out-of-Network.

Premium. The amount an insurance plan costs a policyholder, usually divided up into monthly payments. Employers may pay all or part of this, and low-income families may get a subsidy to cover premiums.

Provider. Any entity that provides health services. May be an individual or a business.

SHOP (Small Business Health Options Program) Exchange. A program that allows small businesses to purchase insurance for their employees at a discounted rate, based on combining the purchasing power of many small businesses.

Subsidy. Money provided to low-income families (or individuals) who do not qualify for Medicare or Medicaid and who must purchase health insurance on their own. Subsidies are not offered to employees to buy employer-sponsored insurance. However, low-income employees may choose to take a subsidy and purchase insurance outside of their employment.

UCR (Usual, Customary, and Reasonable). The price for a service based on locality and prices paid by other providers of the same service. UCR helps set, and justify, allowed amounts.

Urgent Care. A level of care beneath the immediacy of an emergency room but above that of a regular doctor's appointment. Used for medical conditions where a reasonable person would seek care right away but wouldn't need the full range of life-saving services an emergency room provides.

Bibliography

Bendery, Jennifer. "Tim Huelskamp Explains Why 42nd House Vote to Repeal Obamacare Will Be Better Than the Previous 41." *Huffington Post*. Last updated September 16, 2013. http://www.huffingtonpost.com/2013/09/13/tim-huelskamp-obamacare-repeal_n_3921960.html.

Bluestein, Adam. "An Obamacare Glossary: Everything You Need to Know." *Inc.* Last modified February 27, 2013. http://www.inc.com/magazine/201303/adam-bluestein/an-obamacare-glossary.html.

Centers for Medicare and Medicaid Services: The Center for Consumer Information & Insurance Oversight. "Shining a Light on Health Insurance Rate Increases." December 21, 2010. http://www.healthcare.gov/news/factsheets/2010/07/preventive-serviceslist.html#CoveredPreventiveServicesforWomenIncludingPregnantWomen.

Commonwealth of Massachusetts Division of Health Care Finance and Policy. "Massachusetts Household and Employer Insurance Surveys: Results from 2011." Center for Health Information and Analysis. January 2013. http://www.mass.gov/chia/docs/r/pubs/13/mhisreport-1-29-13.pdf.

Copeland, Curtis W. "New Entities Created Pursuant to the Patient Protection and Affordable Care Act." Congressional Research Service. July 8, 2010. https://opencrs.com/document/R41315.

Families USA. "2013 Federal Poverty Guidelines." Accessed October 15, 2013. http://www.familiesusa.org/resources/tools-for-advocates/guides/federal-poverty-guidelines.html.

Gengler, Amanda. "The Massachusetts (Health Care) Experiment." *CNN Money*. June 4, 2013. http://money.cnn.com/2013/06/01/pf/massachusetts-health-care.moneymag/index.html.

Goodman, John C. "Curing the Healthcare Crisis: Empowering Patients and Caregivers." *Psychology Today*. February 13, 2013. http://www.psychologytoday.com/blog/curing-the-healthcare-crisis/201302/how-will-obamacare-affect-health-savings-accounts-0.

HealthCare.gov. "Glossary: Catastrophic Plan." Accessed October 15, 2013. https://www.healthcare.gov/glossary/catastrophic-health-plan/.

HealthCare.gov. "What is the SHOP Marketplace?" Accessed October 15, 2013. https://www.healthcare.gov/what-is-the-shop-marketplace/.

Health Insurance 101. "ACA Provisions: Coverage Tiers." Community Catalyst and Georgetown University Health Policy Institute. Accessed October 15, 2013. http://101.communitycatalyst.org/aca-provisions/coverage-tiers.

Health Insurance 101. "ACA Provisions: Essential Benefit Package" Community Catalyst and Georgetown University Health Policy Institute. Accessed October 15, 2013. http://101.communitycatalyst.org/aca-provisions/essential-benefit-package.

Health Resources and Services Administration. "Women's Preventive Services Guidelines: Affordable Care Act Expands Prevention Coverage for Women's Health and Well-Being." Accessed October 15, 2013. http://www.hrsa.gov/womensguidelines/.

Horn, Dan. "Middle Class, A Matter of Income, Attitude." *USA Today*. April 14, 2013. http://www.usatoday.com/story/money/business/2013/04/14/middle-class-hard-define/2080565.

Kessler, Glenn. "How Many Pages of Regulations for 'Obamacare'?" *Washington Post*. May 15, 2013. http://www.washingtonpost.com/blogs/fact-checker/post/how-manypages-of-regulations-for-obamacare/2013/05/14/61eec914-bcf9-11e2-9b09-1638acc3942e_blog.html.

Kritz, Fran. TakePart. "9 Freebies You'll Soon Be Getting Under Obamacare." May 13, 2013. http://www.takepart.com/article/2013/05/13/obamacare-healthcare-freebies.

Merlis, Mark. "The Affordable Care Act and Employer-Sponsored Insurance for Working Americans." Academy Health. Accessed October 15, 2013. http://www.academyhealth.org/files/nhpc/2011/AH_2011AffordableCareReportFINAL3.pdf.

National Bureau of Economic Research. "Employer-Sponsored Health Insurance and Health Reform." Accessed October 15, 2013. http://www.nber.org/aginghealth/2009no2/w14839.html.

National Conference of State Legislatures. "State Actions to Address Health Insurance Exchanges." Last updated September 30, 2013. http://www.ncsl.org/issues-research/health/state-actions-to-implement-the-health-benefit.aspx.

Obama, Barack. "Remarks by the President at Markey for Senate Rally, Boston, MA." The White House: Speeches & Remarks. June 12, 2013. http://www.whitehouse.gov/the-press-office/2013/06/12/remarks-president-markey-senate-rally-boston-ma.

ObamacareFacts.com. "ObamaCare Insurance Premiums: How ObamaCare Affects Health Insurance Premiums." Accessed October 15, 2013. http://obamacarefacts.com/obamacare-health-insurance-premiums.php.

ObamacareFacts.com "ObamaCare Medicaid Expansion." Accessed October 15, 2013. http://obamacarefacts.com/obamacares-medicaid-expansion.php.

ObamaCare Pros and Cons. "Glossary." Accessed October 15, 2013. http://obamacareprosandcons.org/glossary.

Pagliery, Jose. "Who's the Killer Employee Under Obamacare? No. 50 or 51?" *CNN Money.* May 23, 2013. http://money.cnn.com/2013/05/23/smallbusiness/obamacare-employer-mandate/index.html.

Pipes, Sally. "For Small Business Owners, The Obamacare Reality Bites." *Forbes.* July 8, 2013. http://www.forbes.com/sites/sallypipes/2013/07/08/for-small-business-owners-the-obamacare-reality-bites/.

Ranji, Usha, Alina Salganicoff, and Tina Park. "Access to Abortion Coverage and Health Reform." The Henry J. Kaiser Family Foundation. November 2010. http://kaiserfamilyfoundation.files.wordpress.com/2013/01/8021.pdf.

Staff of *The Washington Post*. *Landmark: The Inside Story of America's New Health-Care Law—The Affordable Care Act—and What It Means for Us All*. New York: PublicAffairs, 2010.

Tate, Nick J. *ObamaCare Survival Guide*. Boca Raton, FL: Humanix Books, 2013.

U.S. Department of Health and Human Services. "State by State." HHS.gov/HealthCare. Accessed October 15, 2013. http://www.hhs.gov/healthcare/facts/bystate/statebystate.html.

U.S. Department of Labor. "Glossary of Health Coverage and Medical Terms." Accessed October 15, 2013. http://www.dol.gov/ebsa/pdf/SBCUniformGlossary.pdf.

U.S. Preventive Services Task Force. "USPSTF A and B Recommendations." Last modified August 2013. http://www.uspreventiveservicestaskforce.org/uspstf/uspsabrecs.htm.

Index

qualifying for, 33, 54
state refusal to expand,
10, 22, 56
Medical condition, denial
of coverage based on, 121
Medical devices, taxes on,
39, 83, 107
Medically necessary, 150
Medical necessity, letter
of, 87
Medical specialization,
rise in, 19
Medicare, 8–9, 40. *See also*
Seniors and current
Medicare users
coverage of insured
under, 35
drug discount to
patients on, 39
expansion of, 27
increased taxes on, 83
Part A, 9, 82
Part B, 9, 82
Part C, 9, 82
Part D, 9, 28, 82
Plan D, 27
qualifying for, 54
reforms in, 83
solvency of, 30
taxes on, 39
Medicare Advantage,
82, 83
Mental health
addiction counseling
and, 125
counseling on, 84
Insurance companies
efforts to drop, 126
Mental health services, 86,
90, 123–126, 143

Medicaid expansion
and, 123–124
private insurance
and, 124
problems with,
125–126
publically funded, 123
substance abuse
services and, 125
Middle-class adults, 110–113
defined, 110–111
employer-sponsored
insurance for, 111
essential health
benefits for, 113
preventive care for, 113
problems with
Obamacare for,
112–113
self-employment of,
111–112
subsidies for, 111
Minimum value, 150
Money flow, 4–5
Morning-after pill, 64

N
National Labor Relations
Board, 7
Newborn care, 143
Newborns
hypothyroid screening
for, 77
phenylketonuria
screening for, 77
sickle cell screening
for, 77
Nixon, Richard
health insurance
under, 11, 18
HMOs and, 13

Nonhospital medical
care, 81
Non-participating states,
Medicaid eligibility
and, 59
Nonprofit insurance, 5
Nurse practitioners, 141
Nursing homes, federal
monitoring of, 28

O
Obamacare, 52
current health
insurance under, 58
defined, 147, 151
differences between
men and women
under, 68
division between 50
and 51 employees as
defect in, 133
freebies under, 55
impact of, on U.S.
taxpayers, 37–38
need for tweaking of, ix
need to be well
informed on, xi–xii
number of pages in, ix–x
objections to, 21–23
passage of, ix
as pejorative term, ix
pillars of
focusing on
preventive care,
20–21
lowering costs
by grouping
consumers, 19–20
lowering premium
costs by pooling
risk, 20

CPSIA information
Printed in the US/
LVOW04s1820\' (11
413333LV00

3 152529